YOUR YEAR
~FOR~
CHANGE

ALSO BY BRONNIE WARE

THE TOP FIVE REGRETS OF THE DYING:
A Life Transformed by the Dearly Departing

HAY HOUSE TITLES
OF RELATED INTEREST

A DAILY DOSE OF SANITY: A Five-Minute Soul Recharge for Every Day of the Year, by Alan Cohen

FOR THE SENDER: Four Letters. Twelve Songs. One Story (book-with-CD), by Alex Woodard

I CAN SEE CLEARLY NOW, by Dr. Wayne W. Dyer

SOUL COACHING: 28 Days to Discover Your Authentic Self, by Denise Linn

YOU CAN CREATE AN EXCEPTIONAL LIFE, by Louise Hay and Cheryl Richardson

All of the above are available at your local bookstore,
or may be ordered by visiting:

Hay House USA: www.hayhouse.com®
Hay House Australia: www.hayhouse.com.au
Hay House UK: www.hayhouse.co.uk
Hay House South Africa: www.hayhouse.co.za
Hay House India: www.hayhouse.co.in

YOUR YEAR

&∞ FOR &

CHANGE

52 REFLECTIONS FOR REGRET-FREE LIVING

BRONNIE WARE

HAY HOUSE, INC.
Carlsbad, California • New York City
London • Sydney • Johannesburg
Vancouver • Hong Kong • New Delhi

Published and distributed in the United States by: Hay House, Inc.:
www.hayhouse.com® • *Published and distributed in Australia by:*
Hay House Australia Pty. Ltd.: www.hayhouse.com.au • *Published
and distributed in the United Kingdom by:* Hay House UK, Ltd.: www
.hayhouse.co.uk • *Published and distributed in the Republic of South
Africa by:* Hay House SA (Pty), Ltd.: www.hayhouse.co.za • *Distributed
in Canada by:* Raincoast Books: www.raincoast.com • *Published in
India by:* Hay House Publishers India: www.hayhouse.co.in

Cover design: Gaelyn Larrick • *Interior design:* Nick C. Welch

**Cataloging-in-Publication Data is on file
with the Library of Congress**

ISBN: 978-1-4019-4608-1

10 9 8 7 6 5 4 3 2 1
1st edition, October 2014

Printed in the United States of America

For my daughter, Elena,
a true bringer of light.

CONTENTS

INTRODUCTION

Although childhood is such a brief part of our overall existence, it shapes the rest of our lives like no other time. In hindsight, it flies by. Yet to a child, it seems to drag on forever. My childhood was no different in these regards.

I was blessed to grow up on a large farm with the freedom to go horse riding or wandering on foot over paddocks for hours. Enormous, endless skies watched over me as I grew into a young woman. With that growth, though, came restlessness for discovery and escape, a feeling that was not to leave me until I finally dealt with my own inner restlessness.

There were certainly many blessings in my childhood. But it was shaped by consistent ridicule, too, the result of being the black sheep of the family. So while I learned independence and developed a deep love of nature, I also carried immense pain into my early-adult years.

From the farm, I ventured to the city to begin a career in banking—in a sensible job, in a life expected of me. However, my restlessness festered, watching me change jobs and locations regularly over the years, until the pain of my life finally drove me onto the artist's path, initially as a photographer and writer, and then as a singer/ songwriter.

It was during these years of growing with my music that I decided to accept a live-in role as a carer for an elderly lady. Little did I know then just how much this work was going to heal me, and how significant it was going to be as a part of my life's work. I will always be grateful for every perfect step of my life, including the pain, that drove me to this work and to the joy that lay beyond.

That first role led into eight years of palliative care, with long, incredibly special hours spent at the bedsides of dying people. I was their carer, there to help their final days be as comfortable and peaceful as possible. Since the people were too ill to be active, the bulk of the time that they spent awake, they chose to talk. And talk they did.

Intimate conversations flowed naturally and openly. The dying don't tend to waste time talking about trivial things. They realize how precious time is, and most use it as efficiently as possible. Luckily for me, they spent it talking from the heart.

Over those years, common themes began surfacing so regularly that it was impossible for me to ignore the messages life was sending. The dying had regrets, and those regrets caused many people immense anguish and frustration at the end.

Looking back on those special years, the theme of regrets was the one that had the most profound effect on me personally. It was too repetitious not to leave a lasting impression. Sure, not everyone had regrets; some people were relatively peaceful and accepting of their life choices. But a lot more had them than didn't.

Despite the regrets coming from all angles, familiar themes surfaced. The most common regrets from the dying people I cared for were:

1. *I wish I'd had the courage to live a life true to myself, not the life others expected of me.*
2. *I wish I hadn't worked so hard.*
3. *I wish I'd had the courage to express my feelings.*
4. *I wish I had stayed in touch with my friends.*
5. *I wish I had let myself be happier.*

My experience in witnessing these in the people I came to love continues to give me strength in making what-could-be-difficult decisions, as I know too well the pain of regret when it is too late. There was so much about living that I learned through the dying.

While caring for Ruth, my first palliative client, I was taught the importance of not making assumptions. Her family dealt with their impending loss in ways that were different from my own personal approach. But I came to understand and respect their choices.

Stella and I were kindred spirits. She was also a wonderful teacher to me. Together we were reminded of the significance of surrender and of how much we all play a role in each other's journeys.

Dear Grace, who became one of the closest people to my heart, taught me through her anguish and regret just how crucial it is to develop the courage to live your own life. I now honor her by doing so every day.

Anthony was a product of his environment, a sad example of who we can become if we don't exercise the power of choice that we are blessed with.

YOUR YEAR FOR CHANGE

Unaware of the teacher role that she played, Florence reminded me of the limits we can create for ourselves through emotional anguish. Compassion and mental discipline then became my catalysts for removing such constraints, allowing me to live with the joy that is my natural right.

John, a wonderful man, was heavy with regret in his final months. He realized that he had placed too much importance on work and had lost sight of balance. I will never forget the sound of his sad sighs as he sat watching the sunset, reviewing his life with a heavy heart.

Positive action and acceptance were two of the things I learned most from Pearl. She had embraced life's lessons well and was a wonderful teacher and spirit. Pearl had also developed great trust and faith in things flowing her way, inspiring others to do the same.

Charlie was a delight to know. Despite his weakness and pain, his spirit remained strong until the end. Simplicity was a message he repeated over and over. Keeping things simple kept life spacious and manageable, he said. He was right.

Open communication was not so easy for Jozsef, who died with the regret that his family had not truly known him. Being honest and open had not been a part of his life, yet he longed to share things with his family in his last weeks. Sadly, he died with much still kept inside.

Jude, who was younger than many of the people I cared for, strengthened the messages of courage, being honest, and living life true to yourself. She was also a great advocate for freeing one's self from guilt, insisting that it was completely wrong and unnecessary in life.

Through Nanci, I was reminded of the futility of assumptions. Despite her illness, which was both mental and physical, she surprised me again and again. We can never truly know what is going on in someone else's head and heart unless they express it themselves.

Dying people wish to live as fully as possible in their final weeks, including enjoying humor when they can. For this reason, staying in touch with old friends carries great significance, and this was a regret for many who didn't. Doris died peacefully after having been fortunate enough to reconnect with one of her friends, although had left it too late to reach others.

Elizabeth was the finest example of our potential for growth and just how much we can change ourselves if we truly wish to. She had transformed herself from a frustrated, alcoholic woman to become one of the best teachers I had the pleasure to know and learn from.

The joy of friendship was reinforced by Harry, who was also a wonderful teacher. He reminded me of the significance of taking time out for happiness, to allow ourselves the balance our hearts so dearly need.

Realizing that happiness is a choice was life-changing for Rosemary, who had always believed that she didn't deserve to be happy. Looking back with regret, she did the best she could to find some peace with her life choices, and began allowing herself moments of happiness in her final weeks. It was a beautiful, heart-opening thing to observe.

Cath was on a mission to emphasize the enormous importance of staying present and developing gratitude for every day. She had missed a lot of her life by always chasing something in the future, before realizing how beautiful the present day really was.

Dear Lenny was a wonderful teacher and such a gentle soul. He was the best reminder I've ever known about perspective. His life had been incredibly difficult with plenty of sadness, yet he viewed it through a wise and accepting heart.

More detailed stories about each of these people are in my book *The Top Five Regrets of the Dying,* along with the story of my own transformation. There is so much to be learned from dying people, and from looking honestly at our own potential death.

What I have learned most is that to live without regret, to have a life you can look back on with genuine acceptance and peace, there are certain values and actions you must honor consistently. To cultivate such a life—and it *is* a cultivation process, one of ongoing growth and nurturing—you must learn to exercise new habits. In order to live without regret, you must work consciously, developing courage, hope, gratitude, faith, honesty, compassion, positive thought, healthy action, trust, presence, acceptance of change, self-love and self-respect, and a heart-honoring attitude.

With these characteristics in mind, I now share with you 52 stories from my life. Each comes with a message, a reminder of these qualities needed to create a life free of regret. The dying taught me that while there will be moments of significant learning through large events, it is actually day-to-day living that is the best teacher. You just need to open your eyes and heart to the messages that life sends. Some of the most significant insights will arise through the most subtle occasions.

Through the gentle and sometimes seemingly ordinary reminders that are presented every day, you will start to see how much you can genuinely own your own life. This is a joyous thing, and it is your right.

These 52 essays are reminders that it absolutely is possible to find strength, develop gratitude, and make the right choices for your life. They are observations made through the footsteps of my journey, but are relevant to us all in the messages that they share. Some of them come from my blog, *Inspiration and Chai*. Others are adaptations from the blog, beginning their journey there but changing shape and direction in their own evolution onto these pages. And many are brand new altogether.

The stories are not listed in chronological order, nor are they in perfect seasonal flow. The choice of order has been a very conscious one, though, to emphasize each story's message while still allowing space for contemplation. Life is full of a variety of lessons, and these are shared from many angles.

The mind will do its best to resist change initially, as you take more conscious control of your life. For this reason, repetition of certain messages is also intentional. It allows the lessons to keep building on each other, assisting you to understand yourself on a deep, soul level.

The book is structured to initially accompany you for one year, with a story for contemplation each week. If you are tempted to read right through instead, then of course do. However, the experience gained through more contemplation on a weekly basis will be much more beneficial and longer lasting. So if you do read right through straight away, it will still bring more benefit to revisit each story again, with more time given to it.

To truly gain from the messages shared and to initiate permanent positive change in your thinking and therefore your life, I suggest you keep a journal nearby. If the message of the essay is about discovering new parts of yourself, for example, then use that week to take notes about your observations. If the message is about compassion, for example, see how that applies to your current outlook and situation. Open yourself up intentionally to the message of the story, find how it fits into your current life, and discover what you can learn and apply from it.

As the year unfolds, you will be treading more consciously along your path, finding strength to make changes, recognizing both the old and new parts of yourself with kindness, and discovering daily reasons for gratitude that may have once gone unnoticed.

Through these observations from everyday life, you will come to understand that it is worth every effort to put positive action and self-love into practice, to create the life your heart is calling you for, and to make this your year for change.

May you come to know the blessing of living without regrets, and even more so, to live the life that you truly are here to live, in joy and wonder.

With loving kindness,
Bronnie

1

A DIFFERENT PERSPECTIVE

While stopped for roadwork a while ago, I sat looking out through the windscreen wipers as they moved from side to side. The rain itself wasn't particularly heavy. But the wind, thunder, and lightning that accompanied the storm as it passed over were ferocious.

Waiting for the temporary traffic light to change to green, I glanced out the side window, into the paddock beside the road. There I saw a very newborn calf trying to stand up, which it did successfully. The mother cow licked it, although the rain ensured it was getting a good wash anyway.

I wondered what it must be like to be born in such a storm, and for that to be the little calf's first impression of life. When the gray clouds passed over and the rain and wind stopped, would the calf wonder what was wrong— why had the sky suddenly turned blue, and where had all the wet stuff gone that was falling down? Would it always be waiting for another storm in order for life to feel regular again, as this was the first world it knew?

Since I live in a valley of cattle and dairy farms, it is not uncommon to see newborn calves, which of course I love. When I then saw another newborn calf on its first day not long after, a day that was hot and dry, I couldn't help but wonder how differently these two little calves would see the world. Maybe they wouldn't actually think about it. They'd be happy just drinking their mother's milk and running around as baby animals do.

Having made friends with various cows over the years, though, I have no doubt of their ability to think and to learn. So I do wonder how different their perspectives on life are and how it would affect each of their life experiences.

A visit to the city called me a few weeks ago. While heading to my favorite tea shop to restock on chai, I found myself walking behind an elderly lady who had osteoporosis or some condition that saw her walking with such a bent back that she was looking at the ground the whole time. She almost bent forward at right angles from the hip.

Naturally I felt a rush of compassion for her, in that she couldn't be looking out at the world as she walked. Then I thought about the little calves and the whole perspective thing. Perhaps the woman saw it differently. Perhaps she was grateful that she still had the independence to be out and about as she wished, when I am sure many her age are no longer able to.

I thought of all of those people, young and old, who are ill or confined and would have happily accepted such a situation rather than the one they were in. People who were too ill to walk, to carry their own shopping bags, or to just enjoy the outside air all came to mind. I also thought of the women I used to teach in jail—I am sure any of them would have changed places with this elderly lady in a moment. She may have had a bent-over back and viewed the world from a different angle from most people, but she had independence and mobility. And she was powering along at a good pace, too.

It doesn't matter how difficult life can be at times. Shifting the perspective can make all the difference. After all, what may appear as a storm to one person may seem a blessing to another.

Seeing life through someone else's eyes can also help you view your own life from a different perspective. This can lift the lid on your own wisdom without your even realizing it, as new answers then flow. It is all a matter of perspective. There are blessings to be found through most situations—sometimes they are just hidden from normal view and need to be looked at from another angle in order to be found.

When I think of that little lady walking down that city street, I am reminded that things are not always as they appear to be. In fact, they are often much, much better.

2

A GENTLE TEACHER

With one of my favorite friends overseas at the moment, enjoying romance, the job of looking after her dog has fallen to me—a job I am more than happy to have.

When I first met the dog, Missy, a few months ago, she had just come to my friend's house at the request of a local veterinarian. Missy had been very badly abused during her brief life and was showing symptoms of extreme post-traumatic stress.

Whenever I visited, my friend had to gently pull Missy over on a lead to get her to come to me. Either that, or we'd have to wait about ten minutes while Missy ran back and forth, wanting to come but terrified to do so, each step coming closer, then running away, then coming another step closer.

Once she was within reach of our hands, she allowed affection and soaked it up completely. In fact, once we began, there was no getting rid of her. She could not get enough of it. Even so, she would be weak in her hind legs, scared to stand to full height, still exhibiting signs of how she had been traumatized, half expecting to be yelled at or beaten—the poor, beautiful thing.

When we stopped and went inside for lunch, the trust gained previously was almost entirely forgotten by Missy. The whole process had to be repeated all over again, with us gaining her trust and confidence simply to pat her and give her some much-needed love, and with her satisfying her own desire to receive that love yet being terrified to do so.

Obviously she came to the right home. My friend has given birth to six children of her own and emanates the loving mother energy without effort. This is just what Missy has needed. In the couple of months since I first met this lovely creature, she has, step-by-step, evolved into a new dog, thanks to the love of my friend. Sadly, there are still signs of her trauma to be seen. She continues to do her dance of running away before coming forward with most people. But her levels of trust grow by the day.

Over the last two weeks, my bond with Missy has strengthened daily, with long walks, lots of affection, and the most communicative eye contact a dog could ever offer. She is a beautiful soul, and what that dear dog must have gone through, I hate to imagine.

In quiet time together, Missy now trusts me enough to roll over completely, so I can rub her belly. When standing, she will jump up ever so gently to be closer to me, putting her paws on my thighs as she looks at me with those beautiful eyes. And for the first time since I've known her, I now see her tail wag regularly as she runs around the yard with me, or whenever I speak with her.

It is such a heartwarming transformation to watch and has truly shown me the power of trust and courage.

Missy is the most courageous soul I have met in a long time. Despite the effects of the hurt she has suffered, she has dared to trust again, to allow love in, to realize that not everyone is like the people from her past.

The unconditional love that dogs give to their companions is a great lesson for us all at the best of times. But seeing Missy's courage in trying to trust again, I think she plays the role of a gentle teacher as well. When she dares to trust, she does not know what lies ahead. Simply that she needs to try to do so, in order to allow love in and for her own happiness.

If only all the people of the world who are carrying trauma and fear from past hurts had the courage of Missy to try again, to open their hearts, and to know that not everyone they are meeting or will meet are the same kinds of people as those from their past.

Seeing this delightful dog wagging her tail and smiling at me with her eyes is a joyous thing to witness. And so is seeing people transform their own lives with equal courage and trust.

3

ACCEPTING
CHANGE

A cool breeze blows softly, and the first rays of the winter sun for the day warm me. Birds sing from trees near and far. Frogs croak in the sunshine, as the creek sparkles in the morning light. From a nearby farm, a rooster crows. No human sounds can be heard at all. It is bliss.

Although change is a part of life, I say thanks for small consistencies, too. The songs of the birds may change. Some of them move on; others stay around all year. The frogs change their song as the seasons change as well, and different frogs share their joy through voice. But in general, the beauty of this farm remains. Any changes actually add to the consistency of that beauty.

My father, already an elderly man, had a major operation recently, and I am reminded of the impermanence of life, of the guarantee of change whether we like it or not.

He is doing okay, hopefully coming through it, but he is old and will never be as he was.

Of course it is not just the elderly who must face change. At all ages we are forced to submit to the natural ebb and flow of life. Nothing remains the same. Those who try to resist and try to control every outcome are often those who suffer most when life throws obstacles their way. Change is always in the air.

I was over at my favorite beach the other day. Walking in the winter sunshine is a joy, with the days so welcoming by late morning. The pool that I have enjoyed numerous times throughout the last two summers was empty of swimmers, the water too cold for even the bravest. I thought about the changing faces of beaches with the seasons rolling around each year. In six months' time, the pool will have swimmers in it from sunrise until after sunset. But at this time of year, it is a smooth oasis, tempting us into anticipating the warmer months.

Whether it is an official seasonal change or not, though, there are seasons and cycles within our own lives. We cannot hold on to one kind of season because we love it more, hoping to stop the others from coming around.

Acceptance of change—whether on a personal, seasonal, or global level—definitely allows life to flow more naturally, bringing new seasons and joys, ones we may never have imagined.

Like a swimming pool waiting to give happiness to swimmers again in the warmer months, I open to the joys of change that are gently blowing my way. And I wish the same for you in your world.

4

ACKNOWLEDGING DEATH

Growing up, I was exposed to life and death regularly. We had to help cows birth their babes at times or bottle-feed orphaned lambs. We saw animals killed before our eyes—cows, sheep, snakes, chickens, and sick horses. Back then, as a child, death was a finality that simply led to an animal decomposing. It didn't occur to me to link it to the mythical heaven I was being taught about at school and in church.

I was also told that God was everywhere and, being raised in a religion that thrived on guilt, would often be relieved when I pulled back the curtains in my room to find that no one was there watching me.

Life has since taught me that heaven is not only for the dying, but is available to us now. Through meditation, I have experienced states within that have been incredibly blissful and beyond the human day-to-day world. Yet such states are available to us even when we're not meditating, by learning to become more present and grateful. Those moments of heightened awareness are there for us all, with overwhelming joy arriving from within.

Animals are of course capable of feeling fear and love. Yet the actual link between death in animals and death in humans didn't really happen for me until I was exposed to the passing of my first patient. Until then, I'd had relatives die but had been kept from it. Unfortunately, this is not uncommon in the society we live in. It doesn't help anyone to deny death. It is time we faced it, in a positive way.

The subject of death, especially in modern lifestyles, terrifies most people. It may be fear of what is or is not beyond this life, or fear of the actual dying process. It can be a fear of having to deal with a subject of such depth. It is often also a fear of facing the fact that life is indeed coming to a close, whether you have done everything you wanted to or not. It can be all of these for some people.

Death brings finality to this lifetime (whether you believe in future lifetimes or not). Denying this is something that we as a society have created, and it is to our detriment.

Let's face it: You are going to die. I am going to die. We are all going to die! Rather than letting this fact be all about doom and gloom, though, you can use your acceptance of death to live a vastly better life. Use death as a tool for living.

You are not here forever. Every day of your life is a gift, even more so if it is a life with the freedom of good health. Either way, it is still a gift, one that will one day expire. Every day that you live is one day less of your life remaining. So why not make the most of this precious gift of time?

It is easy to assume that you will live with great health to a ripe old age, and then die peacefully in your sleep, wearing your favorite pajamas. It doesn't work out this way for most people, however. No one wants to face the fact that they may not live past 60. They may not even live past 40. But this is the truth of life.

History has shown repeatedly that some of us die younger than others. It is not always "other people" either, strangers from families we do not know. It is us. Some people also experience long illness, so the freedom of healthy living can disappear unexpectedly and must be embraced while present.

So with this knowledge, what should you do?

Start creating the habit of counting your blessings for being alive today. Take ownership of your life. Shift your priorities. You *are* going to die! Understand this, and get excited about the gift of today. You are alive right now. Make the most of this incredible blessing of life and the gifts it brings.

In regard to the other fears associated with death, there are other positive things to consider: I have seen dying people beaming at something only they can see, with smiles so glorious that it is obvious they are completely joyous about where they are going to next. They have shown me repeatedly that there is something incredibly beautiful to look forward to. Here lies the idea of heaven, a place or state of love, acceptance, and pure bliss.

Knowing there is love beyond should dispel many fears, although the act of dying itself does terrify some people. Please be assured that the actual death process is quick. Your spirit is not extracted from your body as a tug-of-war game for ten days in a row. It is brief, so not at all worth being scared of. There is also love surrounding you, even if it seems like you are dying alone in this earthly world.

Talking about deep subjects is facing reality. Death does not have to be a scary topic. It may make you sad, to honestly consider that a loved one may not be visibly by your side for every day that is left in your lifetime. But doesn't facing this fact make the time remaining together even more special?

This only leaves the other fear—realizing that there was so much more you intended to do, but now time is running out. So *get on with it,* friends! Make the most of living. Face your inevitable death. Then be grateful for life and your ability to make choices.

Your life is definitely worth celebrating. So until your time to depart arrives, I wish fear-free, honest living to you. Embrace your life. Be joyful. Be courageous.

5

ALLOWING THE SURPRISE OF YOU

When I was 17, my friends threw me a surprise birthday party. I was a bit slow in realizing it, though. They had led me to believe that about ten of us were going to dinner. Instead, when I arrived at a friend's house, about 30 people yelled, "Surprise!" In my naïveté, I just thought that there were more people coming to dinner than I had expected. It took a few minutes for me to understand that the party was here (and to get over my hidden disappointment that we weren't going to dinner!). It turned out to be a joy-filled, wonderful evening of huge laughter and fun, much better than would have been possible at a restaurant.

Despite that slow start, I do love surprises. This is probably a lucky thing, as life brings them to everyone at one time or another. So the more open you can be to change, the less jolting it will be. In fact, the greatest surprise I enjoy is the surprise of who I am, of who I have become.

Allowing yourself to be amazed in this way makes growing a delightful process, rather than one of control and resistance. Joy is your natural state. Yet reaching such a position requires you to be brave and determined, to learn when to soldier on and when to surrender, and to explode the boundaries that have subconsciously been created to limit your levels of happiness. It also requires faith and delight in the positive surprise of who you are and who you are becoming.

As you move forward, one small change and step at a time, old habits lose their strength, becoming less powerful. They don't always give up easily, though. If you find yourself slipping back into limiting or negative belief systems, be gentle and forgiving. It is a process, and one that does not change overnight.

While you are learning new things, marvel at the mystery of who you are, a mystery even to yourself at times. There is magic in the unfolding of a person consciously trying to be the best they can. Smile gently and laugh at new discoveries, allowing yourself to be surprised by how amazing you are becoming. Let it be a joyous process, as best you can.

Who you will become is who your heart has always hoped you could be. It just takes time, love, patience, and being open to the positive surprise of who you truly are. But it is by far the best surprise you can ever hope for. Congratulations! You are on your way.

6

BEAUTY OF A NEW DAY

How beautiful to wake with the natural joy of a bird or of a babe, to wake with no purpose but to sing or laugh for the simple delight of being alive.

It is springtime, and orange butterflies flitter about in pairs. The sun shines brightly through the trees as I sit on my outside lounge and absorb this beautiful morning. The day's heat will surely arrive, and the place will seem deserted under a midday sun. But in early morning, it is fresh and gorgeous.

Even without the innocence and pure trust of a babe, it is still possible to embrace a new day. It is amazing at times how a night's sleep will bring you into a whole new chapter of your life. Of course you never know which night will be that one of restful sleep and positive change. But tears and frustrations of the previous weeks or months are so often washed away at the right time, and you wake looking at the world through clearer eyes and a lighter heart.

You see that the worst is now behind you, that the storm has passed. And while there is still cleaning up to do after the storm, things to put in place, you realize that you now have the strength and energy to do so. Help will come for the cleanup if needed. It is beneficial to stay open to that possibility.

It is important to have had times of rest and surrender, to simply experience your feelings and allow them out. Where would growth be without such times? How could beautiful mornings ever stand a chance of being noticed and savored without the comparison of darkness and storms?

Each day brings the opportunity to sit and absorb the newness of the morning, to realize that you are ready to move forward again. It brings you hope and renewal. Of course it may be some time before you feel like lying on your back and kicking your legs in the air like a babe in joy, or sitting in a tree and singing like a bird, but it is a new day and here you are.

A delightful bird is teasing me. It is tiny and flitting about nearby, but never gets too close. It sings and laughs, leaving me smiling. Insects chatter. My heart is open. A new day is here.

7

BEING FLEXIBLE

It's not unusual to get stuck in routines. Sometimes routines serve you well, but sometimes they don't. At times you don't even know what you are yearning for; all you know is that it is not the life you are living. Then the routines that served you well for years, those that kept equanimity in your lifestyle, no longer work.

Many people are stuck in routines without even knowing why. A man-made clock determines meal times, not the body's clock saying that it is hungry. Morning tea must be at 10 A.M. Lunch is at noon on the dot or heaven forbid. If the 7:36 train is five minutes late, the whole day is out of whack. Saturday mornings are for cleaning house or grocery shopping. Annual leave is at the same time each year.

Things change, though, as do you. So rather than resisting the changes, try to go with them. Be flexible, as the same routine that once served you well may also possibly become the routine that leaves you feeling trapped and unfulfilled.

It is about letting go of the need for total control. I mean, do you really ever have complete control of your life anyway? No. No one does. You may think you do, and then life will throw you a challenge out of the blue that knocks you completely off balance. And you're suddenly looking for a new solution to an unforeseen predicament.

Focus is great, sure. But with that, flexibility is needed. The greatest rewards in my own life, from new circumstances presenting themselves to unexpectedly seeing long-lost friends, have come about when I have remained flexible and open to change.

It is spring in Australia. In this part of the country and farther north and west, jacaranda trees are in full bloom. Each year these lovely big trees brighten up towns and neighborhoods with their delightful purple color, as they are entirely covered in flowers. As the flowers fall, a lilac carpet surrounds their base. For the rest of the year, outside of blooming season, they are considered a reliable shade tree, with large branches covered in foliage. They are beautiful and well-loved trees.

It used to be that the first weekend in October, which is a long weekend here, was the start of jacaranda season. Always. Towns planned festivals and other tourist events around this lilac bloom. But things have changed—they do not always bloom exactly at that time of year anymore. It seems as if the seasons themselves have changed. The jacaranda tree outside the cottage here has not yet bloomed at all this year and it is already November. Last year I noticed one blooming in December.

Life changes, and to enjoy it best, it is easiest to accept this and remain flexible. Just as the seasons cannot be counted on to remain the same, so too is life.

No outcome the world over is ever guaranteed, except for death and change.

So while routine may serve you well in some capacity, so does flexibility. Loosening the restrictions of strict control opens you up to the more natural flow of life and goodness.

Having a day off midweek, or catching up with friends for breakfast instead of dinner, or letting your children pick their own clothes to wear regardless of how much you struggle with their creative choice are all forms of letting go and being flexible.

Flexibility brings surprises and pleasures that can only come about by not being so rigid. So if you are planning on doing your usual thing over the next couple of days, see if you can loosen things up a bit. Ask yourself when else you can do it, and then choose something different to do instead. Or don't choose anything. Just go walking and see how your time unfolds without routine, control, and rigidity.

Daring to step out of self-imposed conformity always brings pleasure and rewards. But until you try it, how will you ever know what those pleasures and rewards are?

8

BEING MISUNDERSTOOD

All of us go through life being misunderstood at least some of the time. How can you ever *completely* understand another when they have walked a different road, with different life experiences? You can't. You can try. You can put yourself in their shoes and develop empathy, certainly. But you cannot truly understand others on every single level, as we are all beautifully unique.

On very special occasions, though, someone does come along who, regardless of differences in life circumstances, understands you well *immediately*—not just in a way that general friends understand you, but someone who gets you, without explanation. They may never figure you out completely, but their level of understanding is a comfort and brings a sense of belonging like no other.

People like this are rare, but at different times you can indeed be blessed to find such connection with a partner, friend, family member, or work colleague. It is important to truly appreciate such connections, as they are exceptional gifts to be sure.

Sometimes, there is a connection with people up to a point. You can see them as the best mate in the world, the most beautiful partner, or whatever, and this feeling can last for years, months, or just briefly. Then one day you see them through clearer eyes and realize that the friendship or relationship is not actually as healthy for you as you once thought.

Perhaps the balance is off, with everything having been on their terms, or you're both growing in different directions, or you recognize that the values driving each of you are conflicting. Regardless, things do change. We are all constantly growing and evolving. And through that, some friendships and/or relationships will survive and some won't. This is a part of life and impermanence.

At times, though, in learning to honor your own heart, you will be misunderstood completely. Those who had you pigeonholed as being one sort of person may then accuse you of being someone else, simply because you don't fit their expectations. Yet all you are doing is giving yourself the same love you give to others.

This can take a lot of courage. Extracting yourself from someone you still care for, but who you know deep down is actually not that healthy to be around, is not always as easy as that person may think it is for you. Such decisions can be heartbreaking, especially when the mind continues to remind you of their other genuinely lovely parts. But the inner voice of wisdom will not be silenced long term. It reminds you over and over of how it is time to honor your own needs and that, despite the history, it is time to let go and move on.

Such decisions don't just hurt the person being left behind. It can be incredibly painful to leave friendships or relationships that had many positives as well. Yet in order to move forward, you can no longer share your feelings on that level with the person in question, or you are back into the unhealthy dynamics of the relationship as it was, on their terms again.

Some relationships and friendships are definitely worth the work. The amazing growth that can come from honest communication and emotional maturity is healing and life-changing in the best of ways. Sometimes, though, your heart tells you over and over that it is time to let go. Breaking the habits of that friendship or relationship may leave you being misunderstood by others, spoken harshly of, or accused of not being the person they thought you were.

You can't control how others will react. If you wanted to do that, you would have to spend your life retracing your steps to ensure that every single person you ever met liked and understood you; still, you would never succeed. This is the nature of the human heart and mind. They have free choice to feel and think whatever they like. You simply cannot control that in others.

You can only do your best to be understood, and especially to understand yourself and your own deepest needs. One of these is to know your own love and to listen to your own heart, even when it tells you to go in directions you know will bring you (and possibly others) pain. Just know that not listening to your heart brings much more pain in the long term.

Honesty takes courage—but so does silence. Breaking patterns, no longer explaining yourself over and over, and knowing that you will be misunderstood are sometimes necessary in order to honor your own heart and health. A friend of mine lives by the motto "Never complain, never explain." I love this, as sometimes explaining takes far more effort than it is worth.

Feel compassion, certainly. But know that sometimes compassion has to be detached, from a distance, with trust that the other person is on their own journey and that you have both played the role you were meant to in each other's lives, in order to facilitate the growth you are both now experiencing, individually.

Letting go is not always easy. But sometimes, it is absolutely necessary.

Staying silent is not always easy either, but sometimes it is just as necessary.

9

BIRDS AND BULL

A willy-wagtail sits on the veranda ledge here as I write. They are delightful birds, and this one in particular has become quite a part of my days.

My life was going through changes a while back, some of which were not completely enjoyable, so the beautiful, stunning environment that I live in was the perfect antidote. On the hardest days, this little bird would turn up and sit quietly nearby. I decided that she was a she, due to her mothering and nurturing senses.

Another day I was on the veranda talking on the phone and burst out laughing with my friend on the other end. Willy-wagtail cracked up as well, breaking into a great joyful song with me. That was the moment I realized how connected this bird was to me. Animals can sense animal lovers.

In the news a couple of weeks ago there was an outcry when a young girl, laughing, threw live puppies into a flowing river. Not long before, a woman had been busted throwing a cat into a garbage bin, and a boy had been filmed throwing a dog off a bridge. The outcry was justified, definitely. It is heartbreaking to see the arrogance of humans in the way they treat other beings. Animals have a right to be here just as much as we do. It is their planet, too.

What prompted me to write on this topic was reading a news article last week about a woman being gouged by a running bull in Spain. The focus was on her being hurt, not on the bull. It is not a natural state for *any* animal to be running down a street, being chased and yelled at. Of course it is going to act irrationally. It is terrified.

So we, as a society, cry out when puppies are injured or mistreated—and rightly so—but why not when other animals are? This continues to puzzle me, although I was delighted to see that there is a growing movement in Spain to stop this awful practice.

It is not a secret that I don't eat meat and am an animal lover. But having grown up in a totally different world from the one I now live in, I do respect that everyone has the right to live how it feels naturally for them. Sure, it would be a beautiful world if animals were not killed, but this reality may be a long way off, if ever.

I don't judge someone if they eat meat. Plenty of people I love do so. The thing that saddens me is the lack of empathy. Most people don't even think about what they are doing. They don't consider the feelings of the animals at all. In a way, I guess I do understand, as the truth is pretty confronting.

The cottage I am living in as I write this story is one of five homes on a couple of thousand acres. Down this end, we enjoy living in a beautiful location as a creek runs by. A mountain on the property offers views across to the coast. After years of house-sitting in places with perfect gardens, it is lovely to be where the length of the lawn really doesn't matter. Wildflowers are allowed to grow, and horses wander in and eat the grass.

There is an abundance of natural life to observe, and one of the loveliest things so far happened last week. Hearing a different noise outside, I looked out—only to see the back of a huge bull that had wandered into the yard. I'd never seen him before, but I was happy for the lawn to be mowed. Spring is here and the grass is growing fast again, after all.

A couple of minutes later, I then heard another noise and turned around to find him sticking his head inside the back door. Now, I grew up with cattle and know that if they are treated well, they can be relatively friendly. But I've never seen a bull do this, let alone one so enormous. I said hello to him so he could hear my voice and wouldn't be frightened by then seeing someone.

He hung around, so I went to the door. He didn't move initially, but when I tried to pat him, he wasn't sure, breathing heavily while making his decision to stay or go. So I sat down in front of him and tried again. With me now at eye level of this huge creature, he allowed me to pat the side of his face. He was still a bit tentative, but when I stopped, he didn't go away. So I did it again, which he allowed. He ended up closing his eyes and enjoying it for a minute or so, then wandered off to eat more grass.

It was about an hour later that I read the article about the woman in Spain, and my heart naturally went out to the bull, thinking how gentle the nature of the bull here was once trust was established.

Walking over the paddocks later, I heard the familiar call of willy-wagtail. She goes with me wherever I walk, and if I don't notice and acknowledge her, she sings out to me. Once I respond, she will then fly ahead to the next fence post and wait. I love it.

When I heard her yesterday, I looked toward the fence only to find her sitting right between the ears of the big bull. If ever there was to be a moment to wish for a camera, that was it.

I thought how naturally birds land on cows and horses, knowing without fear that they will be welcome. Yet very few birds land on humans until a relationship is established. Obviously the collective consciousness of birds has instilled a fear in them of people. You can't blame them, after years of duck hunting, chicken farming, and the like.

The bull wandered back into the yard again this morning. I carried on with my business out there without either of us bothering each other. It was symbiotic.

The natural world continues to amaze me every day in one way or another. Nature has so much to teach us, if we are open to the learning. Even cities have pockets of nature to inspire. In order to maintain true balance, it is absolutely necessary for everyone to spend time in the natural world, in whatever capacity is possible.

I hope the birds are singing in your world, too. If they are, I also hope you notice! We have much to learn through the cohabitants of this magnificent planet, as life speaks to us in many languages. All we need to do is listen.

10

CHOOSING
HAPPINESS

By far, the biggest blessing of my life was conceiving naturally at 44, bringing my daughter, Elena, into the world only two weeks before my 45th birthday. You can imagine how, as a new mother, my life changed considerably from that point on.

Anyone with children knows that parenthood can sometimes be the hardest job in the world. But it can also be the most wonderful. My greatest joy is waking to see my daughter's little face beside me each morning, ready to embrace the world with enthusiasm that is wildly contagious.

This little toddler teaches me greatly about life. It could make me sad to think how free we are born and how restricted we can later become. I choose to be inspired instead, determined to reconnect regularly with the little girl inside of me, too. She is still there, just as the little girl or boy is still inside of you. That part of you knows how to be happy and wants you to know lightness again, to remind you that life truly is a joyful blessing.

So how do you reconnect with natural happiness? You choose to, as simple as that. One step at a time, you make the choice. Despite life throwing challenges and growth at you regularly, what you choose to focus on is still your right.

During my years with dying people, this realization—that happiness is a choice—created one of the most common regrets of the people I cared for. It was heartbreaking to hear the stories people shared, looking back and seeing how they had allowed the opinions of others to shape them, rather than claim their own entitlement to happiness. Even more heartbreaking was their realization that, simply, there had actually been a choice all along.

If you are in chronic pain, suffering a debilitating disease, for example, you could ask, where is the happiness in that? But does a smile still not come your way at times from someone who cares? Is the rest of your body not working perfectly and supporting your other internal systems? Are there not sounds of nature nearby to inspire and enjoy?

Despite whatever challenge life throws your way, choosing to focus on something positive is always a choice you can make. It is not denying what is, as the new thing you focus on is a part of that as well. A bad day or a bad week doesn't have to make a bad life. Feel sad, angry, or whatever needs to be felt. Then choose happiness again.

You also need to accept that you are actually worthy of happiness. You *are* worthy. This acceptance will come through developing self-love, self-forgiveness, gratitude, and, of course, conscious choice. Be kind to yourself.

It is a new start. Find something to make you smile, even if just for a moment. It takes practice, but like anything, you get better with practice.

The crazy thing about life is that it flows best when you are happy. So the happy person creates more "luck" than someone focused on the negative. It is easy to be waiting for a change in your life that will then supposedly make you happy, be it a new job, a new relationship, a new anything. Change arrives in the other order, though: Happiness comes first. The rest then follows. So despite the situation, the only way to make things change and improve is to put in the effort, mentally and physically, to be happier. Smile at strangers, exercise, observe life, and find surprising things to smile at. Your heart will thank you.

Delight is infectious, in the best possible way. Happiness attracts happiness, so the happier you become, the happier you become!

This is your life. Create it with joy, one step at a time.

11

DIFFERENCE
OF A MOMENT

Last night, the rain fell softly all evening. It lulled us to sleep with its gentle patter on the tin roof.

For the first time in a long time, my daughter slept wonderfully. As a result, I woke feeling relatively normal and much more capable than I have in recent times. Everything felt so much more natural than it does in the waking haze that follows months of fragmented sleep!

As the sun rose, it shone clean, unfiltered light upon the front yard. Yesterday, it was all green. Today, after the evening of rain, the lawn was a delightful yellow as the leaves of autumn have begun falling. With a clearer head from decent sleep and a view so different from the previous day, I thought what a difference a day can make.

Tomorrow we hit the road for a short holiday. The difference of another day will be that we are going to be looking at life from somewhere else, from yet another viewpoint. Travel is great for shifting perspective. It is not always necessary to travel, though. Sometimes, even in your regular life, the difference of a day, or even a moment, can make all the difference.

If you have been going through a time of difficulty—a time of growth in disguise—you may finally feel a drop of hope in your heart again. The physical changes may seem gradual, but that one day or one moment, where the drop of hope returned, is when the tides turned.

At other times, the changes are dramatic and you are reminded without doubt of just how quickly life can change, just what a positive difference a day can make.

It may take a particular conversation, a rainy night, or something else tangible, something you can define physically. But it can also take just a subtle shift in your consciousness, for no obvious reason other than you have reached a place of readiness, even if you were not truly aware such readiness was arriving. Suddenly life feels easier again, doable. You feel capable and cleansed.

It helps to remember that times like this do happen to us all. It saves a lot of energy in trying to always work things out. Sometimes you just wake up as a different person, someone with a lighter heart, a bounce in your step again.

What a difference sleep can make for renewal, rejuvenation, and change. What a difference a single day can make. What a difference a drop of unexpected insight can make!

It only takes a moment . . . one beautiful moment of difference.

∂ ∞

12

DISSOLVING
THE EGO

Some years back, I was serving at a meditation center in the mountains that I used to frequent a lot. The place is run by volunteers—all giving their time with the volition that as someone else made it possible for them to benefit from sitting a course on this meditation path, they were doing the same for other students following.

During these years, I served quite often. When I wasn't serving, I was grabbing any stretches of time I could, to sit another course myself. It was a very special chapter in my life, one of healing on an enormous scale.

The role of the server varied, and it wasn't possible to state a preference of duties. After all, we were there with the intention of serving others in whatever capacity we were needed. I often felt blessed to score the role I loved anyway, that of managing the female students. But sometimes it would be kitchen work, gardening, cleaning, office work, or whatever.

On one particular course, I was serving in the kitchen. The person given the role of kitchen manager was a lovely lady, but one who was a senior schoolteacher and very used to telling people what to do. In the world outside the center, such leadership skills were great. But leading a dhamma kitchen was a different story altogether. It wasn't about ordering people around, but rather allowing the kitchen to flow with gentle guidance.

Things came to a head one day between the kitchen manager and a couple of other servers. The rest of us just observed things from our workbenches. (I must digress here. Whenever there were conflicts in the kitchen, the food suffered in one way or another. When I was sitting a course in silence as a student, if a meal came out that had been burned, or if the meals were served up terribly late, we always knew there had been kitchen conflicts. Interestingly enough, when the kitchen team worked together with the right intention, the cooking and food deliveries flowed beautifully.)

On this particular day, the kitchen manager stormed off in frustration and tears to speak with one of the main meditation teachers about the lack of flow in the kitchen. The person whose role it was in guiding the students through the meditation lessons was a beautifully wise woman, appropriately named Grace.

Her only response to the kitchen manager's complaints was that we are all here on this earth to learn how to dissolve our egos, so the best thing the kitchen manager could do would be to go meditate for an hour and see how she felt afterward. She returned to the kitchen as a changed woman, peaceful and accepting. Since compassion is a driving force on the Buddhist path, the other kitchen staff just let things go and got on with it.

Those words from Grace to the kitchen manager have never left me. Whenever I would struggle with a particular issue of relevance, I would again remember that we are here to learn how to dissolve our egos. As soon as I then allowed that choice to unfold in myself, compassion would replace all negative feelings. Really, it is often the ego that stops most people from being able to forgive or to move on from a disagreement—leaving them cemented in stubbornness or having to prove a point.

I am not saying to let people walk over you. I am certainly an advocate for self-love and self-respect, and there are times when speaking up is completely necessary. But so many relationships lose precious time because of the ego, with one or both people feeling too stubborn to let things go and move on.

Sadly, I also saw this stubbornness too often with some dying people and their families. Some people went to their graves with things unresolved, while others were left living with similar fixity. (Thankfully, other dying people also realized the futility in holding on to things because of ego and found peace in long-estranged relationships before dying.)

Dropping the ego and accepting that we all make mistakes is a blessing to ourselves, even more than to the person we are feeling discontentment with. It really does not matter who was right or wrong.

I had lessons in dissolving the ego this week—lessons of a completely different kind, but still relevant. Dissolving the ego is a lesson I actually enjoy these days. I realize the true benefit of it, which is the freedom that comes from working without ego. It genuinely is an amazing feeling.

Some of my articles get reposted on blogs belonging to others. We rarely deny permission to do this if people write to request it, providing that they include a link back to the original source. Occasionally, though, people get carried away. One such case happened a couple of years ago. Someone had changed my article completely, adding his own opinions throughout, then sent it off into the big wide Internet world with my name still on it. It was brought to my attention and addressed in a diplomatic and peaceful way. The writer's intentions had been in the right place, and he had not realized the full extent of his plagiarism. So he corrected things as best he could, by sending out the original article to the same people.

Then there are times when someone will post one of my articles, unchanged, but with their own name on it instead. This happened a few times this week—just one of those weeks for it, I guess. We received e-mails from all sorts of places advising of these injustices. Some messages came from people I don't know but who are very loyal to my writing. Some friends phoned to say that they had received forwarded mail (recognizing my articles, but with someone else's name on them). And some e-mails came from people on my mailing list, for which I am very grateful.

In the modern human world, posting my articles and claiming them as one's own is very wrong. It is definitely plagiarism and can be pursued by law. But on a soul level, I am usually able to find peace with it by dissolving the ego and considering that at least people are still being inspired. The words may have come through me and are based on my own personal experiences, but spiritually, they originate from a much bigger source.

If I can let go and remember that, it is easier to accept that my words are still doing the job they were meant to. It is just my name that is not getting all the credit. But life is crediting me in other ways all the time, through other blessings. And those who are plagiarizing my work have their own lessons to learn. Life will look after them, too, by guiding them through whatever they are here to experience, whether pleasant or not. I do like to think, though, that at the end of the day, most people are reposting the articles with the right intention.

Ideally, credit will come back to me in the long run. After all, I am still an artist needing to earn a living and have that right, through the years of effort I have invested into my work. But often things come to us in ways so unexpected. And the more I can let go and trust that— dissolving the ego and setting legal boundaries, but not losing my own inner peace in the process—the better off I am.

Every day, life offers everyone opportunities to practice dissolving the ego. So much is driven by ego and pride. Yet so much freedom awaits by dropping those things and trying to step back, seeing the big picture instead. It doesn't matter if other people do not recognize your choice and wisdom in stepping back. It is a freedom you can give to yourself.

The more it is practiced, the easier it gets. And truly, dissolving the ego is one of the greatest freedoms I know. There are many gifts you can give yourself. But this choice is one that, in the long run, brings rewards to us on *all* levels.

Surely we all deserve giving ourselves such freedom?

13

DOING NOTHING, DOING SOMETHING

A fridge magnet I once read (which apparently came from a Spanish proverb) said something like "How beautiful to do nothing and then rest afterward." How perfect!

Sometimes it *is* possible to try too hard in life. It can take great strength to let go, surrendering and allowing the creativity of the universe to reveal itself.

Focus and action are definitely needed to consciously create a satisfying life. Your purpose, though, is to ask for what you want and work toward that, but not to control how everything will happen. By obsessing on control, you block the good that wants to come your way.

So comes a time in your life when you may have to wait things out, to do what looks like nothing but is actually something. The act of letting go and staying present, trusting that things are already in place and will unfold at their right time, is a courageous but rewarding one.

In the meantime, allowing oneself pleasure is equally important. Think of a child and the trust they have in each day, staying fully present and allowing goodness to flow their way. This was once your natural state, long before the mind and ego developed imagined fears and got in the way.

At times when you have to let go and take another leap of faith, waiting for things to fall into place, the best thing you can do is to try to enjoy yourself. This is easier said than done, of course. But it brings you to a space of receiving. It allows the good to flow in.

When you are unhappy, scared, in a panic, or knotted up in fear, you are generating energy relating to the fear and giving it more power. When you let go and do something creative, or simply rest, you are nurturing your soul and opening yourself up to all the good that is waiting and wanting to flow your way.

Appreciate the gift of such time—get creative and have fun. Try drawing, cooking, sculpting, writing, music, anything. It doesn't have to be a work of art worthy of gallery walls or five-star restaurants. It is simply doing something you enjoy. It may be lying on the lounge and daydreaming, free of guilt that you should be doing something else.

Like a mighty tree, you grow in spurts. There will be times in which you have rapid periods of growth. This will be followed by times of rest, before the next surge begins. It benefits no one, least of all yourself, to race through life at a crazy pace feeling that if you are not doing something, then you are wasting your time. In truth, you are wasting your time by doing too much.

Take action when it is time to take action. Rest when it is time to rest. Much more is achieved through balance and happiness.

It takes courage to let go. It also takes determination to allow yourself time to play or do nothing, without guilt. Guilt is a poison and serves no one.

Try sitting by a creek, dangling your feet in the water. Perhaps draw something with chalk or experiment with molding clay. Or simply enjoy doing nothing. And, of course, then rest afterward.

Doing nothing is never truly doing nothing. Rather, doing nothing is doing *something,* something very important for both your well-being and your ongoing journey. It allows good to flow. It energizes you and returns some balance into your life. Go on. Give yourself such a gift.

Sometimes, doing nothing is doing everything.

14

FAITH

The autumn leaves have almost finished falling. The chill of winter visits more regularly now. In between, the sun blesses us with occasional perfect days and we head out to the many parks nearby, running through the leaves or simply enjoying being alive and watching others do the same.

While sitting in a park the other day, I watched an elderly man cross a nearby street. He stopped traffic in doing so, yet didn't hesitate to venture out onto the road. He just kept walking, and drivers stopped their cars to let him by. There was a decent amount of traffic, yet he walked out there without a doubt in the world that they would stop for him.

Admittedly, this gentleman comes from a time when people lived simpler lifestyles and were more polite. Perhaps he was still using the same method of crossing the street as when he was a young man, just venturing out there knowing that the drivers would be considerate.

Either way, it left me thinking about the power of faith and how free of fear the man had appeared to be, despite the busy road. He simply knew he had to cross, so he took the first step, then the next and the next. He had the confidence and trust to venture toward his destination, so off he went—and successfully, too.

Children are the same. They trust that their needs will be provided for. They act courageously in almost everything they do, without even being aware of their courage—or more so, their lack of something called "fear." With a loving guardian or parent watching over them, they are correct in their courage. There is nothing to worry about.

Where do adults go wrong then, since everyone begins life as a courageous child? If you managed to stay as confident as the little one inside of you, you would have ongoing trust that life will provide for you. And it would.

Instead, fear is developed, based on other people's opinions of life, the main teachers you come across who tell you it can't be that easy. Such views begin to rule. Your life is altered and shaped accordingly, telling you that you can't do this or that. Before you know it, the ease of flow is almost severed entirely. A new belief system rules now, telling you that life must be hard and that faith is not enough to get you through.

It is, though. Well, faith with action anyway. Those two combined have the ability to truly create everyday miracles, the modern miracle being something happening that could not be planned every step of the way, but was assisted in manifesting by some surprise elements.

Faith doesn't have to be in God, Dhamma, the Universe, or whatever you call the Great Spirit that exists within us, whether you believe in it or not. It doesn't matter. Faith can simply be in yourself, or in life, or in a vision that is so strong that confidence will draw it to you.

On numerous occasions in my own life, the way some things have resulted are so far beyond explanation or possible planning that only my faith could have been responsible in drawing the results to me. Over the years I have taken so many leaps of faith, and despite being challenged, exercising a steadfast resilience has *never* failed me.

Being strong in faith is the challenge, however. As a human, you cannot be strong every day, and this is a part of the test. It is an ebb and flow of strength and surrender. On the strong days, faith carries you forward with an incredible knowing in your heart that all will be well. There is no need to contemplate how or when. Having true faith, you just *know* that it is all going to work out perfectly somehow.

On the days when faith starts sliding, you draw on hope and let that carry you through as best as possible. But what of the days when hope had disappeared, too? At such times, you simply surrender. Let go. Release it. This doesn't have to be a catastrophe. Acknowledge your humanness. Love that part of yourself as well, because from somewhere within, faith will slowly but surely return. This time will pass, and you will find renewed strength. Faith does that. It is a loyal companion once acquainted.

Faith is a talent, a characteristic that you are naturally born with. Yet rarely is it not lost along the way, only to be found again if sought. So it is a skill to be relearned and is best done one step at a time. As you begin to test your faith, stretching your confidence and trust, you become more courageous again, allowing each step to be experienced with more enjoyment and fortitude.

Having faith creates so many possibilities. It quiets the logical mind, a mind that forever seeks answers that don't always need to be found. Faith truly does create miracles. Things may not unfold in the manner you expect, but they turn out even better.

The real work is internal. Your job is to be brave and to bring yourself to a point of readiness, then just get out of the way. Like an old man crossing a busy street, take one small step at a time, never losing sight of your desired destination.

Trust that as each step is revealed, all will be well. This is faith.

15

FENCES

Snow clouds pass overhead, ready to share their load with the mountainous country beyond. The sun breaks through when it can, adding some welcome warmth against the chilly winter breeze.

As I walk back into the village, I notice some guys putting up a new fence, one of green metal. I also pass picket fences, wire fences, wooden fences, brick fences, and hedges planted as fences. People in this village, and most places in the developed world, definitely like their fences. It says, "This is my land. I own it." It can also say, "Don't step past this point without my permission."

In addition, it gives people a boundary for creative expression, knowing that they can do whatever they wish with the land and gardens within this defined boundary. What differences the birds must see as they fly over one fence, then another and another.

Sadly, a fence can also keep goodwill and friendliness out. Many people in the modern world have front fences so high that the home is hidden, and the only way in is to press a buzzer and hope for permission to enter.

I understand the need for privacy, to be able to go about one's day without intrusion. Yet that privacy also blocks out the warmth others may bring.

We don't need to live in each other's pockets, but isn't it a sad thing that more often than not, neighbors don't even know each other these days? A fence, which is just some pieces of metal, wood, brick, or wire, is all that stands between the potential of neighborly good-will or community foundations. Yet so many are scared to even know their neighbors because, heaven forbid, you may get along okay and then have to say hello again another time!

Some years ago I did a six-day walk over farmland in Western Victoria. Permission was given by the land-owners for us to ramble along at our leisure. We were blessed to experience the feeling of eras gone by, when walking was the main means of transport and movement was not hindered by land ownership or barricades. Those six days still affect me positively in many ways years later.

There is an Australian former-politician who lives in Tasmania who has a sign on his rural property saying TRESPASSERS WELCOME. He has a fabulous attitude, allow-ing others to tread gently on the land he caretakes, let-ting them share in the enjoyment of wandering through such beauty.

Fences can block goodness out. But they can also be ignored or overcome, by passing some homegrown vege-tables over them, or some chocolate cake, or even just a word of cheer now and then.

In this busy world we have created, community has been somewhat lost. It is starting to emphasize its own importance again, though, in subtle ways. One of the easiest methods to help that sense of community develop again is to know your neighbors.

Fences may always go up to identify this land-ownership thing that we as a developed world seem to need. But fences can be overcome with a simple hello now and then.

A smile or a wave can go a long way, too.

16

FLOWING
FORWARD

The creek overflows once again, as the runoff from two days of heavy rains flows into the catchment. The bridge is almost covered, too, so I am stuck at home (I love this fact).

There is a part of the creek where it splits into a few smaller streams, then comes together again. It makes me think of life and decisions faced. Watching the creek tells me that you can choose various ways to go, and obviously the journey will be different whichever way you choose. Yet it ultimately all leads in the same general direction, at least for a while, until the next moment of choice arrives.

So when faced with huge or small decisions, there is always free will. But there are some things you are destined to experience and move toward in your lifetime. The choice is in which way you go to get there. Do you choose the apparently easiest or quickest way? Do you take the slow, scenic route? Or do you face the challenges straight on

—taking the bumpy road but getting to the other side with more strength and insights into yourself, making the journey beyond that so much more worthwhile?

The water flows on and comes together. Then farther downstream, it splits again and goes off in a variety of directions. Some of the original creek joins other creeks to become a mighty river, eventually flowing strongly down to the ocean. Some of it continues to join other small streams. And some of it stagnates, coming to a point where the flow has stopped completely, at least until another major rainfall. Then off it goes again, too. Eventually it ends up where it is meant to, as do you.

You shape your life by the decisions you make. Just like the creek choosing to flow one way or another, you too are given free will and may choose which route to take on your own journey. Yet regardless of the choices you make, you continue to move in the right direction for your soul's learning and evolution. There are just some things you are going to learn about yourself, no matter what.

Sometimes, like everyone I am sure, I can make decisions quickly and clearly. At other times, some things need much contemplation. There are times when the answer is not clear and the best thing to do is to simply be. By not forcing an answer to come, it is allowed to reveal itself at the right time . . . and it does.

Then there are times when the answer is just to make a decision. That is the actual answer; that one cannot delay or put one's head in the sand in denial. There come times in everyone's life where one truly does have to make clear choices. Sometimes the decisions that have been brought to the forefront of your life, awaiting your answer, are the biggest ones of all—and, therefore, often the most painful. But just as making hard choices can be painful, so is living a life untrue to yourself.

When faced with some major decisions, there may be moments when you want to ignore them, willing them to go away. But of course they don't go anywhere. So wait until the answers reveal themselves to a calmer mind. Then you can move forward, trusting that the decisions you have made are the best ones for your soul's journey.

The creek bubbles over rocks and reeds, going off in new directions, always ending up where it is meant to, just as life is flowing in the right direction for your own evolution. And even though you may hit a few snags and detours along the way, you are still flowing forward. Trust that it is all for your best in the long run.

Decision time comes around to us all. Eventually, you simply have to face the choices and trust where they take you. It's all growth. It's all evolution. So at the end of the day, really, it's all good.

17

FREEDOM

One of the best things about being Elena's mother—besides the sound of her little voice or giggle, her wonder at everything, her jumbled vocabulary that doesn't stop, when she lifts my shirt to blow raspberries on my belly, or when she crawls onto me to go to sleep at night—is watching her absolute confidence to be herself. She is free.

We all start off like this, and for those of us who consciously choose to live a life true to ourselves, much of the adult years are spent trying to then recapture something similar. The scale of this task is determined by the weight of conditioning received in the years since, the pain associated with breaking free of habits and beliefs that no longer serve us (if they ever truly did), the courage (or lack of) that is able to be mustered up along the way, and the realization of self-worth needed to carry us through the most turbulent waves.

Freedom comes in many forms, physical and emotional. You can be free physically but still be bound emotionally. Until you are free emotionally, you will never truly be free. The path to this complete freedom is self-love, with all of its layers, angles, lessons, insights, and beauty.

If you live with a kind heart toward yourself, you will also live with a kind heart toward others. If you live with a kind heart toward others and not yet to yourself, the journey of self-love awaits and looks forward to your company.

The more you give yourself permission to do things that speak to your heart's desires despite fear, the more practiced you become in giving and receiving your own love. And believe me, it is a beautiful kind of love.

There are many blocks to overcome in the process, most rising to challenge you just as you're breaking through yet another layer of loving yourself. It is easy to sabotage yourself at such a time, knowing that although the other path is more painful, it is familiar.

But you know what? It is okay to be you! It is okay to be brave, wonderful, and *happy*. It is okay to live a life that makes complete sense to you. You are allowed to be you.

What is wrong with cheering out loud down a busy street, just because you're happy and you can? Nothing!

What's wrong with choosing not to work a 40- to 60-hour week but following your heart instead, even though you don't quite yet know the final destination? Nothing!

What's wrong with choosing not to explain yourself to people who have already judged you, without them truly knowing you or the full story? Nothing!

What's wrong with jumping on a trampoline until you're exhausted, laughing and carrying on as silly as you like, even if you're 50 years old? Nothing!

What's wrong with becoming the person you have always dreamed of being? Nothing!

What's wrong with being you? Nothing! Nothing! Nothing!

If you dream of change within, it is time to start allowing yourself. Even with family commitments, it is possible to make positive, self-loving choices. Everyone in a family benefits from the happiness in others as the joy is shared even more. Authentic relationships know and support this.

You are free to choose. You are free to honor your own heart. Exercise that right often. It is your life. You are free to be you.

18

GRATITUDE

During my years as an aspiring singer/songwriter, I was fortunate to meet some fabulous people, including some who were fairly famous in the Australian music industry. Considering that I was never a particularly strong performer myself (unless I was playing at folk clubs, where I seemed to bloom), these were great opportunities for learning, being able to mingle with performers of the highest level.

During a conversation with a man called Todd, who had known massive international fame with his brother and their band in the 1980s, I mentioned how I had messed up a recent gig of mine, making a mistake in a particular song. Todd just shrugged, smiled, and said, "There's always the next song."

He was right. Why ruin a whole gig staying focused on what went wrong with that particular song? It was such a simple sentence, yet it changed my attitude toward performing immensely. Not only was I then able to let a mistake go immediately, giving a fresh start to the next song, but I reached a place where I could just laugh with the audience if I made an error. After all, it wasn't the end of the world, and we are all human.

Being given that simple snippet of advice left me grateful for hearing the right words at the perfect time. It enabled the shift I needed. I was grateful for the advice, of course, but it also moved me into a place of deeper gratitude in many other ways. I began to say *Thank you* for a smooth song prior to the next song being performed. I added *Thank you* into my thinking numerous times throughout future gigs—*Thank you for the song going well, Thank you for the connection with the audience, Thank you for the opportunity to have music flow through me, Thank you for the creative expression of songwriting,* and on it went.

As a result, my pleasure in performing increased, which then enabled the audience to experience more enjoyment. I removed myself from the equation considerably, and things flowed much better. If I did make a mistake, which was not nearly as often, I even managed to be grateful in some way for that, for the learning it offered.

Every day, life gives opportunities and gifts that are worth saying *Thank you* for, even those that may initially leave you feeling uncomfortable. The uneasiness I used to feel while onstage taught me so much about myself and living, so it was always a positive thing, even if in disguise. Now when I am onstage speaking or singing, I can enjoy it, as I am such a different person from who I once was. I could not have become her, though, without first walking those beginner steps.

Life is very good at stretching you as far as you can go, and then stretching you just a little more. Despite how painful this can be, there is *always* a gift in the learning, something that will reveal another layer of yourself. And as the big picture of the human journey is simply about learning and loving, there is no way you will not grow and benefit on some level from such stretching.

Of course, there are also more obvious things to be grateful for, things that can often be taken for granted in everyday living. Developing the habit of gratitude not only opens the flow of more goodness to you, but it brings happiness as well. A grateful person is a happy person. Creating the pattern of saying *Thank you* for what you have now is the path to true abundance. *Everyone* has things to be thankful for.

Are you breathing? Then be grateful for your lungs and the air nourishing your body.

Has someone smiled at you recently? Be grateful for them crossing your path.

Are you well enough to live independently, even if you choose not to? Be grateful for that freedom.

Do you have access to fresh fruit? Be grateful to the earth for providing so magnificently.

Do you have choice? Be grateful for a free mind and the intelligence to use it.

Would someone notice if you died? Be grateful that you are not completely alone.

Do you have fresh water to drink? Be grateful for this essential life force.

Have you laughed lately? Be grateful that you are able to do so.

It is a beautiful life. It is the life you have created. Gratitude makes everything easier. It lessens the challenges, adds a shine, and attracts more positive people and situations. It is the key through any locked door.

I am so thankful for making mistakes onstage and for being reminded of simple things, like that there is always the next song and it is okay to make mistakes and gently laugh at your humanness.

There is always the next minute. Use it well. As you smile and thank life every day, it will also express appreciation right back to you, in increased blessings and joy. Give thanks. Your life truly is worth living.

19

GROWING IN COMPASSION

One of the greatest lessons that life has *ever* taught me is compassion. Since this learning has now become such an integral part of who I am, I see examples of compassion everywhere. This warms my soul and lifts my heart. There is much craziness happening in this busy world we have created. But to witness people still caring for each other is reaffirming that despite occasional appearances, we are, as a species, naturally good and kind. Some have just lost their way.

Compassion is kindness, sympathy, consideration, and especially empathy—the ability to put yourself, as best as possible, into another's shoes to feel the situation properly. Thomas Merton, a gentle and wise scholar from last century, best describes it as the "keen awareness of the interdependence of all living beings." It is wishing for others to not be suffering.

It is a human emotion, yes. It is a powerful force when applied, though, generating loving energy to whomever it is directed to. It also provides the giver a feeling of love from within, an opening of the heart.

Compassion has the power to turn everything around. If you are able to view life from a compassionate place, you let go of the ego and its need to be right, working from the heart instead. This is choosing to be emotionally mature, letting go of the need to validate.

There is already a little compassion in us all. Some of it just needs help being released. Instead of carrying on after a disagreement, for example, where you and the other person lose valuable time from the relationship due to stubbornness, hurt, or not forgiving each other, you can choose to look at the situation from a place of compassion instead. It doesn't mean that you necessarily agree with the actions of that person. It means that you make a conscious choice to not carry that energy with you anymore.

By choosing to look at a situation with compassion, you are more able to look kindly toward others, to see their own frailties and to recognize your own. We are all simply trying to be happy and avoid suffering. No one is immune to learning, making mistakes, or having said or done something that has hurt another. Whether we consciously choose to or not, we are all learning, constantly.

If you can remove your ego from a situation, eliminating your need to be right and seeing the other person's opinions or words as an expression of who they are now—that is, as a result of all they have been and what they have experienced up to this point—then the situation naturally softens immediately. You don't have to agree with everything. Compassion is not about being walked over and trying to be a martyr by saving others. It is simply recognizing that all of us have goodness and all of us have humanness, which at times shows up in less favorable or desirable ways.

When others are speaking unkindly, they are not in their natural space. We are all born as loving creatures with our hearts wide open. Through years of wounds and fears, though, we may sometimes act from a place disconnected from our own true wisdom. So you may have forgotten the loving person you truly are, or the person speaking to you in an offensive way has forgotten who they are. You each have a choice as to how you respond, however.

You can add more suffering to suffering by causing hurt, or you can choose to come from a place of emotional maturity and view the situation through compassionate eyes. The ego will rear up and try to hold on. As you are now working from the heart and not the head, the ego is losing power, which it does not like. But over time, as you grow and develop in compassion, it becomes a natural state for you. It gets easier with practice.

I grew up in an environment where forgiveness was a constant lesson for me. Even though I endured emotional wounds that took years for me to heal, forgiveness was the only way forward. How did I do that, when I had become so fragile, sensitive, and fearful of exposing myself to more of the same, year after year? It wasn't until I was able to develop compassion that things began to change. And they changed enormously.

Through compassion, you learn not to take things personally, because it is really not about you. It is the other person's suffering that they are dumping on you. So if you are able to detach in a loving way and realize that no matter what has been thrown at you, it is really just a manifestation of the other person's hurt, then you are able to have compassion for that person and let it go. This not only stops giving more power to negative situations, it allows healing to begin on all levels for everyone involved, including yourself.

Whether it is the person serving you at the supermarket or an impatient driver on the road, it doesn't matter. There are opportunities to develop and grow in compassion every single day. It takes work to drop the ego and not want to get the last word in, or to be kind to someone who may reject your kindness. Make it about them, though, not you. You can then wish kindness toward them and move on, knowing that the power of compassion is in place and is a force well beyond human comprehension, generating the change needed. It is a loving energy that permeates every area of your life once developed.

So how does one begin to grow in compassion? How do you develop it? Compassion has to start with you, to you. This is the most difficult part of the whole compassionate journey. It *has* to start with you. You can be your own harshest critic, but until you learn to be kind and compassionate toward yourself, you cannot grow in it for others. As Westerners in particular, we can be incredibly harsh on ourselves. Yet we are all children of God, whatever you conceive that to be, and we are all born with the desire to be happy.

You first need to forgive yourself for things of your past. By continuing to carry regret or guilt, you hold yourself back from blooming into the person you are here to be. Sure, you would have done some things differently given the chance, but you are human and you are constantly learning. So forgive yourself and realize that you did what you did as a result of who you were at that time. And you are not that person now. Have compassion for the person you were.

You are constantly growing, constantly evolving into a better person. So be kind to yourself and remember that that was the best you could do back then, as who you were at the time. Be grateful for the growth in yourself that now recognizes this. You must learn to be gentle with yourself. It is the first point of healing for you and for all who come into contact with you.

It may not be easy initially—I cried many tears when I first started generating compassion toward myself. This is not the same as dwelling in the victim mentality, though. It is recognizing and acknowledging the suffering of your own past and generating kindness toward yourself as a result. It is also choosing to love who you were and who you now are. It is about loving all of you.

The power of compassion is a tangible force, with results unimaginable. It is a force of love, forgiveness, kindness, and healing. We all suffer. We all yearn for happiness. We are all capable of healing. Never underestimate the power of compassion. I have seen it heal on all levels of society.

Simply make the choice to be aware of compassion, of it being an option for how you respond to others. But first and foremost, it is an option for how you treat yourself.

The power of compassion needs you on board. Start by generating some toward yourself: Recognize your beauty. Love you, with all of your frailties and mistakes. You are worthy of this love. You are an incredibly beautiful soul with much to share.

When you are able to be kind to yourself, you are then able to be kind to other people, to animals, to the earth, and to all who need compassion along your path. With an open heart, the power of compassion flows through you as naturally as the air that you breathe. You owe it yourself.

Be aware of this magnificent force and all that you are capable of being.

Be kind. Be sympathetic. And above all, be compassionate.

20

HOPE

While deciding to write about hope, I was interested to find that one of the meanings the dictionary gives for the word is "confident desire." Another was "likelihood of success." Still another, more understandably, was "wish or desire."

Funnily enough, when most of us draw on hope it is not necessarily with confident desire. It is faith that contains confidence, the inner knowing that you are on the right track. Even though you may not know how something will unfold, you trust it will.

Hope, on the other hand, often comes with a prayer or uncertain yearning. It is a glimmer of faith but not necessarily with confidence. However, it is only by holding on to this beautiful emotion of hope that the "likelihood of success" can result, particularly if faith is weakening or absent.

With practice, faith can carry you through anything —it is the unwavering belief that something is possible, the magnet to attract what you dream. But there are days when you are not strong. After all, change flows through life as naturally as the air you breathe. So during periods where you are trying to return to a place of faith and certainty, you draw on hope.

It keeps the light of your dream alive. It is an act of surrender, but not one of giving up. It says, "I still want to believe this is possible, but I'm not feeling strong enough to do so today. So I am handing it over to hope, rather than giving up altogether."

That openness allows you to loosen the reins, to let go of control, to be at mercy to the greater forces that have heard your prayer from the very inception. Hope opens the flow in a more vulnerable yet receptive way. It hands it over without losing sight of the dream.

Hope carries your prayers with childlike trust. It is not always with "confident desire." But it is such a tangible and loving force that it certainly carries with it the likelihood of success.

I love hope, and I thank it for carrying me through some of the most difficult times, when faith was on a temporary holiday.

If faith is out of sight in your world today, please visit the world of hope. It is a soft, nurturing, warm blanket that will keep you safe through the stormiest of nights.

21

IMPORTANCE OF HONESTY

More and more as I observe relationships, whether they be friendships, family relationships, business dealings, or romantic partnerships, I notice just how few people have the courage to be truly honest with each other.

More often than not, those who are silencing their honesty seem to do so to keep the peace. But how is peace truly kept if one person is not able to express their feelings honestly, without risking a dose of the other person's wrath? That relationship, therefore, is not on equal, emotionally mature footing, but rather under the control of one person.

Such relationships may still bring pleasure in other ways. Much of the discontent tends to be hidden; that is, until things fester to a point of needing expression. Then it may come to a clash, and what could have been expressed honestly, in a peaceful manner at an earlier time, is now expressed in anger. As a result, any opportunity for understanding or being heard properly is lost immediately.

Is it not better to express yourself honestly as the feelings arise, rather than avoid them to the point when they can no longer be communicated clearly, due to the accumulation of residual feelings that now accompany them?

Of course, there is no guarantee that you will get the reaction you hope for either way. But at least you will have your own respect by communicating honestly. Sometimes you just have to let go and accept that not everyone is in your life permanently. People do come and go. You share the learning you are meant to and move on, sometimes naturally and smoothly, sometimes in a blaze of glory.

Honesty is not always an easy thing to share, nor is it an easy thing to hear. You don't have to agree with what the other person is saying, though, just as they don't have to agree with you. But being respectful of the other person's feelings and honoring the relationship enough to be willing to hear the person out allows for healthy, mature growth in any type of relationship.

If the honesty has been heard and no reconciliation can be found, then it is time to move on. Bless the other person on their journey, whether they know it or not, and let go and move forward. Space will be created in your life for more like-minded people to now enter. Most of all, you will know that you have honored your own heart by being honest. Just because the other person does not like what you have said does not mean you should not have said it, and vice versa. Either way, everyone has a right to be heard.

It takes courage to be honest in any kind of relationship, and sometimes choosing the right timing helps. But what sort of quality is it if one person carries so much power and anger that the other person cannot be themselves? Is that sort of relationship truly worth holding on to anyway?

I have found honesty to be one of the most liberating elements in life. It lets go of unhealthy situations and associations that are no longer good for your well-being, and allows those other beautiful, mature relationships to grow to new levels and bloom.

No one is perfect, and you may not always like what others have said, or even what you have said. But at least you earn your own respect by having the courage to express your feelings.

Honesty can be delivered with compassion and empathy, but those acts of kindness also belong to you. By being honest, you are being compassionate and kind to yourself—and that, of course, is the most important thing of all.

22

INTERNET
CONNECTION

It is an absolutely glorious morning here. Autumn, my favorite time of year, has rolled around again. As the nurturing sun shines on the mountains, I feel incredibly grateful that I have brought my life to this point, where I can do most of my work from home, enjoying the seasons in the process.

Lately I've been thinking about the benefits of the Internet and how much my life has improved as a result of the connection it brings. The Internet is very much a part of most of our lives now, although I do know some people who still live completely free of it, happily so.

If you maintain balance with it, the Internet is a wonderful tool for access to information, for learning, for entertainment, and for what I most love about it: connection with like-minded people. It is when imbalance occurs that the benefits are lost, as with any imbalance. Internet addiction, whether to games, pornography,

Facebook, or whatever, is like any addiction. The user has lost some connection with real life and feels they need the escape from reality, fulfilling underlying needs with superficial ones.

Another thing is that the anonymous nature of cyber-space allows some people to behave in ways they probably would not in real life. It gives a false sense of power that is unfortunately used in negative expression and unkind behavior—behavior not likely to be expressed with face-to-face contact. It is an ugly side of the Internet.

On the positive side, though (the angle I prefer to view life from), this era of technology has brought the world together in countless good ways. Our access to information is simple and efficient. Artists are no longer hindered by corporate interests; they can create their own chan-nels of sharing instead. The world is a smaller place now, with countries far less isolated as in generations gone by.

Yesterday morning I had an interview with a jour-nalist in New York. We were two mums working from home, connecting about motherhood and being writers, even if in different capacities. It was a very sleepy Sunday morning in this country village. The sound of birds sing-ing was all to be heard. It was Saturday evening in the journalist's home. In the distance I could hear New York traffic, and marveled at how two such different worlds could connect with such ease and enjoyment.

So now I sit here on a beautiful Monday morning in Australia, looking at the yellow autumn leaves sprinkled across the yard, seeing the mountains bask in the perfect sunshine, feeling a slight breeze coming through the win-dow, hearing birds singing, and I write to you, in another country or town, another lifestyle, another world.

Yet a friendship and connection exists because we have access to technology, and collectively, we have drawn each other into our lives, through similar philosophies and values. Who would think that something as cold and sterile as a computer could actually generate an infinite amount of positive energy around the world in so many ways?

It is a gift to all of us, a tool to better our lives in whatever way we are guided. Use the resources available and reach out to other like-minded people. Generate positivity. Spread goodwill. The world is indeed a smaller place now, in the best of ways.

23

INVISIBLE MAN

The Invisible Man was a show on television in the mid-1970s. As a young girl, I used to love it; today, I still think about it at times. For example, when I am on an open road with no cars in sight for miles and miles, and I merge in without indicating. I almost always apologize to the Invisible Man, in case he was in the other lane (in his invisible car, of course), and I made him have to swerve. He never honks, though, so I guess he must be a fairly patient driver.

Over the years I have often imagined borrowing an invisible suit, although the Invisible Man himself was actually invisible and wore a visible suit. I have provided myself with much cerebral entertainment in the process, and my desires during such mental escapades have been varied. When I would look after more than a million dollars in cash during some of my days in the banking industry, for instance, the invisible-suit idea certainly came to mind. But alas, I went on earning low wages and disconnected from the actual value of this paper I handled. (You tend to do that in banking.)

Naturally, there have been ideas about spooking friends or being like a fly on the wall during work or personal scenarios. Then if you didn't agree about something that was said, you'd simply mutter, "Rubbish," and freak everyone out as they looked around for where the voice came from. A little mischief here and there can't be a bad thing.

When I first started performing, I yearned for that invisible suit often, sometimes even midway through a song. "Sorry, folks, I just have to put on my invisible suit here." A guitar exits the stage alone.

If you are ever hassled by a maniac on the road, you simply slip into your invisible suit and drive on. Then when they get beside you to yell abuse, they don't know who to yell at and drive off totally bewildered, hopefully retiring from the road-rage profession forever.

I am sure that I would be tempted to put the invisible suit to good use, too. Like letting caged birds fly free, opening gates and removing animals who are suffering from cruelty, placing beautiful signs of encouragement about for people who need it, or planting a soft kiss on the cheek of those I love. While such a suit would definitely make all of this much easier, one can still be clever and bring goodwill to the world without being totally invisible. It only takes timing, a bit of strategy, some courage, and a little mischief.

So if you've not done anything silly lately, or you've not done something kind for a while, start scheming and see what you can come up with. Leave little surprises about for people you love, or even for strangers. It benefits all, those receiving from your actions and you, because it feels great. Fun people are needed in this world. The more happy people we have in our human family, the more happiness the family has as a whole. Get creative. Get mischievous. It is fun!

And don't worry. If I ever see some invisible suits at a clearance sale, I'll be sure to let you know.

24

JUST BE YOURSELF

An immense challenge we are all up against is to be ourselves. Many people don't yet know who that is and, sadly, may never reach their full potential in this lifetime.

To be you takes incredible courage, for two reasons. It means there is a good chance you won't fit in with the "normal" of society, the conditioned majority (at least until we are *all* being ourselves). It also means that you will have to face yourself and your deepest fears to discover who you truly are. To do this takes undoing the conditioning of your past and of those who have influenced you, a combination of family, peers, and society in general.

A couple of years ago, I received an e-mail pointing out that one of my articles had grammatical errors, along with a warning that there are some pedantic critics out there. It was sent with kind, and perhaps nurturing, intentions, so from that perspective, I do appreciate the sentiment. As a person already in the public arena, however, I have come to learn that there will always be critics.

That is the nature of human life. We will never all agree and are entitled to individual opinions.

Do these things, like perfection and faultless grammatical correctness, truly matter in the end, though? I cannot imagine my dying thought being *I wish I would have written that article differently.* I do enjoy improving as a writer. I enjoy improving in any field. But in my heart I am happy by expressing myself honestly. That is all I ask of myself—that, and to enjoy the process of growth that accompanies it. The grammar police may not agree with my style, but they don't need to.

There are tools to help us all in whatever our endeavors may be, and many are worthwhile. Learning is a magnificent thing. We can also learn a lot from each other, definitely. But my heart does feel for those who would write, draw, speak, paint—or *anything* in life—with the concern of how their creative expression will be received. What a weighty burden to bear.

All of this left me thinking, as I wandered these glorious hills and paddocks, about how many people accept conformity as being normal. It is a fearful society we have created as a species, when the majority find it easier to be guided by conformity, even if it brings them no true happiness.

Where is the space for individual expression in such a society? It takes a huge amount of courage to honor your own heart. I don't deny that. And for many, finding the strength to do this can seem too overwhelming and much more difficult than plodding along with the majority. Yet when you hear a beat that works in time for you, knowing that it doesn't match the beat of the majority, you will always be out of rhythm with yourself if you do not learn to honor that beat.

Most people just haven't found their own beat yet. So they walk to that of the collective, even if true happiness is not found by doing so, particularly when the collective is coming from a place that has lost its heart and authenticity. It is also a beat that does not work together.

What an incredibly beautiful symphony it will be when we all truly walk to our own beat. It will be a joyous and perfect tune, all of us happily honoring who we are, working together to create an uplifting, harmonious symphony.

That is where the need for courage comes in, to walk to your own beat. What others think of you is nothing compared to what you think of yourself. So the challenge faced is to honor that deep longing, to realize your true self. It is also the greatest gift you can ever give to yourself and to the world.

When you do this, you then naturally want to contribute to a better world, so everyone benefits from your efforts. Breaking out of others' expectations of you may leave you hearing a barrage of criticism for a long time, while others adjust. But in the end, that criticism is not about you. It belongs to the person or people delivering it. Let it slide, and if you're strong enough, use it as a tool to grow in compassion for the other person's own suffering.

When you start to create your own life, it triggers fear in others. You cannot control that; but you *can* control how you react to these opinions and how much you let them affect you. Stay focused and true to your own heart. It is definitely worth it.

No one has lived the same life as you. We all walk in different shoes with different life experiences. No one, not one person, has ever perceived the world through your eyes. So how on earth can someone else's truth be your truth? It cannot be. You must find your own sense of self—the truth of what drives *you*, of what makes *you* happy.

The opinions of others are based on their own life experiences, and while some may prove relevant and helpful to you, many won't. So take on what you resonate with and filter out the rest. It is the only way. Otherwise you end up remaining who others want you to be, rather than who *you* want to be.

The restraints of conformity are never going to be healthy companions for a happy life. There is a dream within you, slowly beating away to its own rhythm. It wants to be heard. But it cannot be so if you don't slow down your mind and your life enough to hear it. When you do, you will always know it is there. Your peace lies in learning to walk, and eventually dance, to that beat. Happiness is the reward.

Be yourself. It is who you are here to be.

25

LEARNING SELF-LOVE

As I watch my gorgeous little daughter smile at herself in the mirror, my heart opens at her honest expression of self-love and admiration. If I ask her if she is beautiful, without hesitation, she'll reply, "Yes," which of course she is. She can laugh at herself, knowing when she is funny, admiring her own sense of humor, as well as loving her appearance and all of herself in its perfection and magnificence.

Self-love begins as a natural state of living. Why wouldn't you love yourself? You are a divine being of love, perfect as you are in each moment, here for a human experience. Very sadly, though, this natural state of self-love is often lost in the years that follow early youth. Comparisons, self-judgment, and opinions from others lacking in their own self-love can all wear you down, until it is easier to live in self-loathing than to proudly love who you are. How about practicing kindness toward yourself instead?

It is a mistake to put self-love in the same category as selfishness, yet it happens all too often. This misguided judgment hinders people from honoring their own needs, treating themselves with love, in the belief that it is selfish to do so. Let me be clear here: *It is not selfish.* Selfishness is about caring only for yourself. Self-love is about caring for yourself as well as others.

Not only is it not selfish to grow into self-love, it is essential if you wish to make a true and balanced contribution to the world. Instead of self-love creating isolation, as selfishness does, it actually creates union, happiness, and compassion. The ripples that flow from a person comfortable in their own love benefit thousands.

Why, then, is it so difficult to practice this? Is it fear of ridicule, since admitting your own love can attract condemnation from those who don't understand, those who are so far from loving themselves that they cannot even comprehend the idea? Is it a belief system, planted as a young child, that says you are not worthy of good? Are you just too busy to even consider the fact that you don't yet love yourself? Is guilt attached when you think about the things you would do if you truly loved yourself, like taking some time out for your own enjoyment and dreams?

Love in any relationship is an ongoing evolution. Love with yourself is no different. It takes years of kindness, conscious choice, forgiveness, compassion, nurturing, and patience. And as with any journey, there are times it will flow easily and times you need to let go and rest. There are also many parts of you to learn to love, or to remember to love, both past and present.

Love that little child who created misguided belief systems in acts of self-protection. Love the teenager who was finding their way, given some freedom of choice, yet not always knowing how to use it well. Love the young adult who was still shaped by the conditioning of their past. Love the somewhat older adult who may have questioned it all and found pain and sorrow, but kept trying to find their way. And then love who you now are, or will yet become, for the courage in trying to grow into who you were actually born to be.

In order to become that person, there are parts of yourself that need to hear farewell. Do so in love, though, as it is a gradual process of letting go. But you cannot be who you are while still being who you were, particularly if that is a person shaped dominantly by past or current influences of family, peers, or society. Self-love is about giving yourself permission to discover who you really are, and then to work toward honoring that person.

Rather than live with the pressure of unrealistic expectations, give yourself a break. Treat yourself as a child under your protection. Look into your own eyes and say, "I love you," with a gentle smile, and then learn to receive that love. Tell yourself, "I love you," and then demonstrate it. Receive that beautiful love back into your own, tender heart. Be kind to yourself, with gentleness and patience.

The benefits of living in a world where more people have learned to live in self-love are immense. Self-love disintegrates judgment, false expectations on others, impatience, criticism, and pressure. Why? Because a person who walks the path of self-love understands that we all experience suffering at some time and has compassion for that. A self-loving person is a happy person, and a happy person has a lot of joy to share. A self-loving person understands balance, and that sometimes you need to take time out for your own needs in order to be the best you can be for others.

Learning self-love can be the most difficult lesson of all. You deserve your own love, though. So look into the eyes of the person before you, the person you currently are, and with a soft, kind heart, say, "I love you."

It is an ongoing journey, but it all begins with those three words and the warmth of a gentle smile.

26

LESSONS FROM
A CAR PARK

This valley is at times like an empty desert with its silence. Around the middle of the day, the only summer sounds are the insects. Birds are resting in the heat of the day—yet, as usual, their music starts the morning off and returns by midafternoon.

Last night I was watching the antics of a few different types of birds staking out territories and hassling each other, and I thought that even birds seem to have egos at times. It does seem that way, but I'd prefer to put it down to mothering and protective instincts, to give them the benefit of the doubt.

For us humans, though, life is a constant lesson of dissolving the ego and cultivating the heart. A prime opportunity to grow in this department was given to me the other day in a car park.

After a brief trip away, I was heading home, tired but happy. Stopping at the fruit market, I cruised on in, chose a parking space, and proceeded to reverse into it. I drive a van, which is cumbersome (but it also has a bed in the back, which is freedom!). Having learned to drive on a tractor at age seven, I consider myself a pretty good and patient driver.

There were a couple of people walking about, who I saw. But as I had my indicator on and was in the driving part of the car park, I reversed in. The next thing I knew, I was being shouted at by a pedestrian for almost running her daughter over. The daughter was a teenager pushing a shopping trolley, old enough to possess her own common sense. It is not the same as seeing a toddler running wild in a car park, where of course you would stop, even if they were walking in your way.

Receiving anger out of nowhere took me by surprise, so I didn't do anything. The woman stormed off, still yelling abuse at me. Once parked, I hopped out of the van and was about to head into the market, when I thought something along the lines of, *No, this is not acceptable.* Although in my humanness, I'm not so sure my thoughts were *quite* so polite.

It is easy to excuse others' behavior through compassion, and this is the path I usually try to choose. However, there are times when compassion and kindness for yourself have to rule. So I walked over fairly calmly to the lady's car. Her husband was there and puffed up in defense the moment he saw me coming. Sadly, the teenage girl did the same, a product of her angry parents. I asked the lady, calmly, what else I could have done. When she pointed out that I was heading into one car space but changed my mind, I was happy to tell her honestly that I had never intended to park in front and mentioned I had my indicator and reverse lights on.

"So let's just put it down to a misunderstanding, shall we?" I suggested, rather than fight her anger with unkindness or more anger. She was so full of rage over such a small incident that she just screamed some obscenity in reply, then said, "Yes, let's," all the while showing me her very best scowling face.

While my heart was beating like crazy by the time I walked away, I was glad to have addressed the situation. An elderly couple nearby had seen it all, and as I was walking into the market, the old man told me I had handled it well and that the angry woman was in the wrong. This offered some comfort, although it then reinforced how much we can use validation from others to justify our actions—just as the angry woman's validation from her husband justified her own.

Nearby, a guy about my own age was sitting in his small truck. He also commented along similar lines, with understanding and respect. I said thank you, smiled, and headed into the shop. While grabbing a few things, I wanted very much to think compassionately about the three of them, mother, daughter, and father. But my ego was still a little fired up, thinking, *How dare they?*

Within about ten minutes, I was driving home along a beautiful country road when a rush of compassion for them all came through me. I felt sad for the teenage girl who had already become such a product of her parents. I thought of the woman in sisterhood and felt sorry for her, from one woman to another. Obviously she was having a bad day, but I sensed she was probably also having a bad life. The man did what any father and husband would do, puff up in protection of those he loved.

The image of them driving off, all wound up in their rage, came to me. I had already managed to remove most of the angry people from my life over the years. My earlier life had exposed me to enough of it to last more than ten lifetimes. So it wasn't like I was new to anger.

Now, driving past rivers and creeks, with beautiful mountains on either side, I thought about those three people in the car park. They were so connected to each other in their patterns of anger that I wondered what their lives must be like. How could I not feel sorry for them? My heart went out to their misery. Yet I was also peaceful, knowing that I had treated myself kindly by not taking it on, by speaking up for myself. Compassion doesn't mean you have to be a doormat to others. We owe ourselves love above all else.

I guess I could have said nothing and developed compassion for them regardless. That would have been a noble act, totally devoid of ego if done with the right intention. Yet I am still human. And I found that the whole incident was actually a lesson in self-love for me more than a lesson in compassion—though of course it was that as well. Had I responded to the woman in anger, I would have ended up taking her poison on, too. But by managing to stay calm and speaking in the manner I did, a totally different outcome came about.

Car parks in summer are never the most joyous places to be anyway, as fuses run short in the heat and busyness. It is the same case in any retail location near Christmas, really. People lose patience in crowds and are under even more financial pressure than usual. So if we are able to dissolve the ego a little, it saves adding any more fuel to the fire at this busy time.

That evening I was able to sleep well, after a lovely sunset from the veranda, some guitar and singing, then frogs and stars coming out in abundance. The car park felt like a lifetime behind me. Yet I wonder now, as I remember the incident, whether the not-so-happy family also slept well. Or did they use each other's anger to further justify their right, carrying the memory much longer than necessary?

On this occasion, there was a fine line between dissolving the ego, by coming from a place of compassion, to also treating oneself with love. Dissolving the ego and cultivating the heart are ongoing lessons for us all, layer after layer. But the further along you get, the more natural this becomes, as negative reactions thankfully weaken and disappear. While it obviously benefits everyone, even the angry person, if we are compassionate toward each other, the biggest rewards are actually for the giver of compassion themselves.

So during these busy times, I wish you egos that don't rule *too* much. May you also remember, though, that you deserve your own love and compassion. And if this sometimes means speaking up, so be it.

The car-park incident left me with peace and self-love. It left the other people with anger.

I know which I would prefer.

27

LETTING IT BE

If a dog is standing at a fence barking, chances are it would do almost anything to get out of the yard and enjoy the freedom. Yet this morning when I was out walking, a dog was barking to get back *in* to a yard. It was a chilly morning, so perhaps the lure of a cozy cushion by the fire was even more enticing than the adventure of freedom that had come from a fence-jump in the night. Thankfully, the dog was heard and the gate opened. In it ran, wagging its tail, full of fun and gratitude.

Letting some people into your life is not always as easy as that, though, despite it being clear that they want in as much as that little dog wanted in the yard. If someone has hurt you repeatedly over time, a part of you naturally wants to build a fence or a wall to further protect yourself from the risk of more pain.

This coping mechanism comes from a place of hurt, often developed over years, based on belief systems that may no longer serve you well. Rather than putting yourself in the position to risk being exposed to similar behavior, your efforts now go into keeping the person or people out. This can take a lot more energy than you realize.

When I looked after dying people, one regret that surfaced from them regularly was the wish that they had been more courageous in expressing themselves, that they had been more honest. As you find your bravery and practice honesty more often, you improve speaking this way, until it becomes easier and easier, a more natural extension of yourself.

But what if that honesty is expressed and you don't receive the reaction you long for? This is when you realize that the release of expression was actually for your own healing, not necessarily also for the benefit of the other person. It *can* open healing on both sides and often does, but not always. For some, hearing such expression is too confronting. Speaking in detail about their past actions, particularly if they are ashamed of themselves and are yet to reach a place of self-forgiveness, is simply too difficult.

On occasion, too, some people genuinely do not understand just how much pain they have caused. In these cases, your need for expression is often consuming, as you want them to know *how much* they hurt you. To make them accountable for their words or actions feels like it could ease your own pain. It takes a lot of compassion and courage to let go at such times and remember that it truly doesn't matter in the end. Life is the best teacher. The person may not suffer through consciously knowing the pain they caused you, but any seeds sown in life reap their results in one way or another. You don't need to be the vigilante and fix things in others. Life catches up to everyone.

Sorry is a huge word. It can mend years of pain in a brief moment. Hearing it can be the sweetest music ever.

For a relationship that is ready for mature communication from both sides, honesty is the catalyst for much healing and for the magic of the word *sorry* to be shared, sometimes from both of you.

If the relationship has not evolved into a balanced place, though, allowing for that mature and honest communication on both sides, waiting to hear *sorry* could easily be one of the worst wastes of time you could ever spend. Perhaps the other person *is* actually sorry but finds it easier to show it than say it, therefore avoiding more painful confrontation.

Releasing the need to hear *sorry* and allowing another person to communicate their feelings in their own way is a gift of liberation to yourself. Actions can exhibit their remorse louder than the spoken word. As long as you remain trying to control the whole situation, waiting to hear them say that they're sorry, it is your energy lost and your pain that remains.

Sometimes you just have to let it be. Reaching the place of readiness to do this may take much healing. The decision to either let them back in or let it go is yours to make—you can give up your own fight. Despite its potential difficulty, it is also an incredibly beautiful gift to yourself. It is a gift of freedom.

Life is the best teacher, for both of you. You don't have to become best friends overnight or ever again. It is also possible that a part of you may still love them. Whether you decide to love them from a distance or allow them back in to your current life is up to you. You can love someone from afar or silently, secure in the knowledge that in order to also love yourself, you need to be away from that person.

However you do it, there often comes a time in life when you must make a choice to let them in again or let them go. Either way, making that choice releases the energy previously given to keeping them out. It can be hard work, to be sure, but it will also be healing and bring relief. It can stop you from having regrets at the end of your life, too, by not allowing your pain to dominate your whole life. It takes dissolving the ego, forgiveness, and compassion . . . most of all, though, it just takes a decision.

Like a dog with a wagging tail, desperate to come into the warmth and comfort of a loving environment, allowing others in brings relief and gratitude in ways still unimagined. Then as *you* relax by the fire, safe in the comfort of simplicity and peace, life suddenly feels much less complicated. And sometimes, letting go of the struggle is the gift to yourself, a time of nurturing.

Let them in or let them go. Either way, it is time to heal. Let it be.

28

MAGNIFICENCE

Some time ago, while connecting with readers on my Facebook page, I asked them to share some of their favorite words with me. Naturally, asking such an open question did leave room for a couple of dubious answers, which were promptly deleted. The joys of social networking!

Overall, though, the replies were fabulous, leaving me smiling and inspired as I read through the list. Some people wrote about the sound of words they loved, like *bumblebee*, which I agree is wonderful. Most people wrote about words that had significance to them, like *breathe, humor, magical, kindness, sunshine,* and *believe*.

When I was first learning to write songs, I realized one day that by changing just one word in the lyrics, you could change the mood of the whole song. That is how powerful words are, both individually and when combined into sentences and conversations.

There are various words that I have loved over the years, including *joy* and *convivial*. My most favorite word these days is, not surprisingly, *daughter*. Another word that I have loved for a long time, and one that seems to be rising in prominence and usage, is *magnificence*.

Magnificence is not about buildings or man-made structures, though it can be if you wish. Magnificence is about your true self, the authentic part of who you are, your fullest potential when you let go of all that holds you back. Magnificence is who you truly are when you dare to be who you truly are. It seems crazy that this is where the real work in life is: to be yourself on all levels, without hindrance of others' expectations or your own judgments. Yet it is in fact where the actual work lies and where the genuine rewards await.

Why, then, is your own magnificence so frightening? Why must fear or guilt accompany your desires to live your dreams, to honor your heart, to enjoy life? It is only because you allow it to. Do you dare to be truly happy without explanation to others, without their under-standing? Yes! Indeed! It starts by *allowing* yourself to do the things you love, and to let your magnificence shine through the joy that then follows.

God wants you to be happy, to celebrate living, to know your own magnificence. If the lessons attracted into your life are seemingly contradicting this, look for the positives. The big picture will always reveal gifts given with any test. You are loved. Every challenge is an oppor-tunity to return to your own magnificence, to honor your own heart, to know happiness on a more authentic level. Your main job is to enjoy life, without guilt, judgment, or justification. You are allowed to be magnificent, joyous, and blissful.

Be present and see where life guides you, rather than trying to control every step of the way. Smile and reveal yourself *even to yourself* on a daily basis, rather than having a fixed image of who you are, one that you may currently present to both yourself and to the world.

You are allowed to change. You are allowed to let go.

Magnificence. It is who you are when you are free of your own judgments. It is also who you are when you are free of others' expectations. And it is who you are at the very core of your being. It is who you *already* are. It is now time to joyfully show this to yourself and to the world.

It is time to allow your magnificence through.

29

MEDITATION

Sitting in a darkened room, with no awareness of anything outside of my body, my mind lets go into somewhere new within itself. This is one of the wonders of meditation—when we let go completely, the mind reveals yet another layer of itself, a place of incredible beauty, free from busyness and thinking.

Finding my way to a path of meditation has been an enormous blessing. For years I read books and tried a little meditating based on what I was reading. Some good guided meditations came my way, too, via cassettes and eventually CDs. Yet all through these years, despite my intention and determination, I never truly believed that I was capable of mastering my mind. Instead, I welcomed the brief time-out that these meditations gave me, using them for relaxation, affirmations, or intentional manifesting.

The idea that the mind was actually trainable still enticed me, like some exotic country that I believed existed, but never really thought I would visit in person. Meditation kept calling to me—it was a magnet with a slow, subtle pull, drawing me home into myself. Ultimately, I found myself in a hall in the mountains, trying to master the practice while sitting in excruciating physical pain, surrounded by a hundred or so other people who, like me, had committed to ten days of silence.

Vipassana meditation had always fascinated me. Out of ignorance, this fascination was mainly due to the novelty of trying to live for ten days without speaking. I had no idea then how much I would actually come to treasure the silence, and that the technique itself would be such a catalyst to lift the lid on my necessary healing.

When I finished my first ten-day course (though at the time I would have said "survived" it), I thought to myself, *That was fine, but I'm never putting myself through that again.* And I believed it. I walked out of there grateful for the experience, but with no intention of ever going back. Yet a year later, almost to the day, I found myself back in the same hall, sitting in similar excruciating pain, wondering how on earth I had ended up back there.

A few months later I served on a course. The center is run by volunteers consisting of old students, anyone who had already sat at least one course. It was during these ten days of service that I realized Vipassana was indeed my path, and that the technique had already helped me to access the tools I was looking for to master my mind. I wanted more. In subsequent years, I spent considerable time sitting more courses in silence as a student, and other courses serving the students who were sitting. But even without being at the center, meditation remains a vital part of my everyday life.

There are many great modalities of meditation available, and we each need to find our own. The signposts will show the way to the right path, as they do for all who seek. One of the things that puts many a beginner off meditation is that after one or two attempts, they're certain that they will never quiet their mind, that their mind alone is just too busy and untrainable. I was once like that myself.

Practice, commitment, and determination definitely do bring improvement. The first time I picked up a guitar, for example, I was so disappointed I couldn't play it immediately that I didn't pick it up again for almost another decade. Yet it also kept calling, and eventually I accepted that becoming a guitar player would be a life-long discovery, one that I was finally ready to begin and enjoy. Such is the case with meditation. Such is the case with being human. It is a journey.

When we commit to mastering the mind, it initially fights back with incredible strength. After all, the mind and the ego have ruled unhindered for your whole life so far. They don't surrender easily now that the heart and the wisdom of the soul are taking over. But to access those truest parts of yourself, one little glimpse at a time, takes focus and strength. It is a lifetime quest.

Like any challenge faced, unexpected rewards can arrive out of the blue, too. It may come as a realization that you are making more conscious choices than in days gone by, or when you catch yourself thinking more positively, or breaking old patterns. Eventually, you find yourself naturally operating from a more conscious place. This is a result of meditation and of learning to own your own mind.

If you have considered trying it, or have already tried it but found it too difficult initially, please remember that the meditation path, like the path of the artist, the musician, or the human, is one that does take a lifetime. It will always be ongoing.

Sometimes you will move forward well. Other times, it will feel like you are getting nowhere. So rest when you need to, then move forward again when you can. Be kind to yourself. There is no race. There is no time limit. The sooner you begin the journey, though, the sooner you can enjoy the delights it offers. You must just begin; take that first step, then another, then another.

If you have been thinking of embarking on a new venture, why wait? *Now* is a great time to begin a journey. If not now, then when?

30

ON THE PLANET

Although I am not as involved with the music scene as I once was, due to changes in lifestyle and career directions, it is still wonderful to be able to reconnect with musician friends as they pass through town. Much of the last ten days have been spent doing just that, at a local music festival.

One such friend put on a great show, and we enjoyed his delightful songs. He and I have never been terribly interwoven in each other's lives, but take delight in catching up whenever our paths cross. There have been the occasional lunch or cups of tea along the way, but generally, we just catch up through music events.

As he sang, I thought about our association with fondness. I acknowledged that while neither of us has any burning need to be more entwined in each other's lives, it is still lovely to know that he is on the planet. And I told him so in parting.

Later, I thought about other people like him in my life—people I don't see often, yet a mutual fondness, respect, and happiness arises when we do cross paths.

It makes me glad to know that they are on the planet. There are so many lovely people I have known briefly over the years, and it brings me joy as I think of them going about their own lives. Just knowing that they are out there somewhere brings warmth to my heart, and I cannot help but send them cheerful thoughts.

It is easy to think in a lateral way, in which your world consists of what you see and what influences your life directly. But in thinking about other good souls, it opens you up even more, bringing a quiet joy. You don't need to be in touch with them by phone or e-mail. You don't need to see them regularly. Some you may never see again. Nevertheless, they are out there, adding to the flavor of this wonderful group called humanity. It is encouraging to be reminded of this. It helps to feel a stronger connection to everything.

We can be bombarded with so much negativity in the media. (Why must bad news carry such sensationalism, I wonder?) Yet just reminding yourself that there are still plenty of decent people out there, too, even if you only met briefly years ago or you just know of them, brings you back to more of the goodness of life.

It also brings me pleasure to know that those who connect with my work (whether through reading my books and articles or listening to my songs) are on the planet. If you connect with my message, then in some way, you are a like-minded soul. I am glad to know that you are on this earth.

Thank you for being a part of this wonderful melting pot of humanity. The world is a better place as a result.

31

ONE STEP AT A TIME

My nana, my father's mother, was a little woman with a strong personality. (Both of my grandmothers were tiny; both stood under five feet tall.) Nana lived in a run-down old house at the back of an overgrown block. I remember only a few things about that time in my childhood: We were never allowed to leave a crumb of food on our plates—we had to lick it clean. There was an avocado tree in the front yard. She always had candies beside her bed.

And there were these old, worn, sandstone steps leading up to her home. The steps were uneven, but I loved them, as they were cut from the rock decades earlier. Their imperfection made them perfect to my child mind. Alongside the path leading up to the steps was a sandstone wall that seemed to tower over me, though in hindsight it was possibly a mere four or five feet high.

Although there were probably only about ten steps in total, they seemed like a long and mysterious climb, as I could not see beyond the top step from the first few lower steps. What lay beyond could have changed each time, according to my uncluttered imagination. There was always a sense of magic and wonder when I would see Nana's rickety old house again.

Likewise, you cannot always see where steps taken in adult life are leading. Sometimes the path appears clear, so you feel confident to proceed. But how do you know there won't be a surprise hazard along the way anyway, even on a path that appears to be so easy and clear?

One step at a time is the only way to go. As long as you have the bravery to keep taking each one as it appears, even if you cannot see every step beyond, you are still moving in the right direction. It takes courage and faith, but it also gives room for flexibility, positive surprise, and a little mystery. Dealing with just one step at a time allows you to become more present. You open further to opportunities that present themselves as you go, rather than rushing headfirst toward a goal, missing the helping points along the way.

The path may wind here and there, but flexibility can be a joyous thing. Letting go of the need to control every step is freedom that assists the journey. Surrendering is not a hindrance at all—it is daring and positive. Being rigid and trying to control every single step, with no openness to the goodness of surprise, is usually the hindrance.

Flexibility and faith go hand in hand when manifesting dreams. Faith holds the dream and vision strong. Flexibility leaves room for positive surprise. The courage to travel this way then attracts unexpected rewards.

The journey begins with just one single step, followed by the next, then the next. With faith and courage, it is not necessary to know what lies beyond, only that it is a path that honors the songs from your heart.

A passage can be hindered, or worse, not even begun, if one thinks too far ahead. So just take the first step, then the next, and allow the creativity of the journey to reveal itself in the best possible ways.

May your eyes and heart be open enough to enjoy every step along the wonderfully mysterious path you tread.

May your journey be blessed, one step at a time.

32

PERMISSION GRANTED

My love of walking long distances started early. Farm life offers children great freedom. It gives space to walk and run, without dangers of traffic or hazards. As a result, a love of walking and open spaces has never left me.

As a young teenager, I ventured out one afternoon across the paddocks for a walk. At some point, I decided to change the direction and head to a friend's place instead. This was farming country, with dirt lanes bordered by massive gum trees. My friend lived a couple of farms over, about an hour's walk away, so off I went, cheerful and carefree.

When I arrived home a few hours later, my mother was distraught. They had been looking for me everywhere, having driven over our paddocks and the surrounding roads in the search. I was reminded that if I was going to go walking off the farm, I needed to ask permission. It hadn't crossed my happy teenage mind to do that. I'd simply made a choice and done it. It wasn't difficult to understand the need to ask permission, to save my mother concern. I respected this in future cases, but it did make me look forward to having a life so free that I didn't need to ask for *anyone's* permission.

Of course, it is usually for our own good and safety that parents put these rules in place. But all children dream of this freedom at some time—of making their own choices and not having to answer to adult caretakers. Adulthood finally arrives, and that freedom is indeed yours. There is no need to ask for anyone else's permission to do what you wish.

But what happens if having such freedom is terrifying? Obviously, some freedoms are easier to adjust to and enjoy than others. Initially, you may find bliss in the thought of living without limits set by another. There are often existing limits still in place, though, set by yourself unconsciously. You then venture further into adulthood, collecting more influences from the opinions of others along the way. Over time, these self-imposed limits can therefore surface and increase.

As you work toward your dreams and feel your way into them, these limits will block them from flowing. Until you realize what the restrictions are, the dreams remain blocked. They are there, waiting and wanting to arrive in your life, but they need permission. More important, *you need to give yourself permission to receive them.*

It is surprisingly easy to sabotage dreams through fears. Rather than focus on the wonders and happiness that may accompany the dreams being realized, subconscious fears from childhood can surface. These can lower your expectations and push the dreams away. It may be fear of others' reactions if you do finally get what you want, or it may be that you don't actually know how to allow it through.

Yet always remember that when it comes to yearnings of the heart, *what you want wants you, too.* It wants to be in your life. It wants to help you become the joyful person you have the potential to become. It wants you to know your own wonder.

Just as there can be times in life when you reach your limit with sadness or challenges, knowing that you truly cannot take anymore, happiness can receive your limitations as well. Eliminating those boundaries is essential in order to truly welcome your dreams in. When you hit these barriers, take the pressure off yourself. Be vulnerable. Ask for help and pray.

You cannot be strong every day. Admitting that you don't know what to do, that you don't know how to give yourself permission, clears unblocked energy. Ask your angels to teach you how, and then allow yourself some unpressured quiet time. Such moments are both vital and healthy. They reconnect you with the wisest part of yourself again, ultimately returning natural strength to you.

As you release resistance and admit that you need help, you open yourself up to receiving. You are actually beginning to give yourself permission even though you think you don't know how. The willingness to acknowledge that your dreams are not here yet, due to self-imposed limitations, is an act of bravery. That vulnerability not only opens you up, but it also clears the way for your dreams to arrive.

You deserve your own permission. There is no sin in wanting what your heart desires. Nor is there sin in wanting an easier life or in wanting happiness. It wants you as much as you want it.

All that your dreams are truly waiting on is for you to reach the place within where you can smile and say with both courage and vulnerability, "Permission is granted."

33

POWER OF CHOICE

We are all given the power of choice. Life is full of decisions and is created daily by the countless choices made. Some of these decisions are conscious, but most are unconscious.

Making conscious, rather than unconscious, choices ensures that you maintain equanimity in your life without the extremes of living unconsciously and being at the mercy of all that comes to test you. You may try to avoid ever making choices or changes, but life will still force you forward. Nothing stays the same. Changes forced, however, rarely happen gracefully. They can leave you feeling like you have no choice. But having decided not to choose previously was also a choice.

Inner growth is a part of life, the process that continually reconnects you with your soul. You can change how you react to challenges by the choices you make, creating a smoother flow and more space for happiness.

Deciding to acknowledge that times of suffering bring with them great opportunities for growth lessens the pain. While you may naturally look forward to when the storm has passed, you can also decide to make it easier on yourself by looking for the gifts that are on offer during the storm. Then when the sun does come out again, you are stronger, renewed, and more connected with yourself.

No one says that choices are easy—nor is ignoring yearnings of the heart. And while actually honoring your heart does not exempt you from growth, a little light will always break through on occasion, continuing to brighten the way.

Whatever choices you are faced with, it is usually fear that is holding you back. It could be fear of what others will think of you, like you've ruined their expectations. It may be fear of the unknown, or fear of failure. Strangely, one of the biggest fears is the fear of success.

True success is being able to give your time to doing what pleases you. This can be alone or in the quality company of others whom you like and respect. Success is knowing that your heart is happy and that the world is benefiting from your being here, no matter how small that contribution may feel. There is no need to be frightened of such a life!

So, you live with the choices you make. What is it that you want? What is it that your heart is truly saying? Is fear stopping you from hearing your heart's voice? What is your biggest dream, and what is stopping you from pursuing it? Is it money, time, or fear? Keep in mind that fear also represents a shortage of time and money: fear to step off the treadmill, fear of lack, or fear of finding new ways to approach life, to learn to see it from a new angle.

You can learn to attract what you need by choosing to get more educated about it. Or you can get more creative in finding solutions. Or you can choose to replace your fears with trust, by facing them and, in time, dissolving them. Best still, you can do all of these.

You have the choice to face and overcome your fears, whatever they are. You have the choice to follow your dreams, whatever they are. You have choice, and life blesses those who take action.

What is your heart saying?

The choice is yours.

34

RAIN AND
GRATITUDE

Despite being in the same region for most of my childhood, I grew up with contrasts of weather.

Almost every summer the banks of Goonoo Goonoo (pronounced "Gunny Ganoo") Creek would burst and flow up through the paddocks to our house. If we were not fast enough with sandbags, the water would flow on inside. Thankfully, there were usually warnings from farmers farther upstream of the floodwater approaching. My folks would evacuate us until it subsided. In fact, it became common for the local newspaper to publish photos of us children on the tractor, being taken out through the floodwater to safety.

Our next farm was struck by severe drought, lasting most of the decade. While school friends headed off to the beach with their families, our holidays were spent sitting on the backs of horses in the scorching summer heat, minding the sheep as they fed off the sides of the roads. There was no longer any grass left for them in our own paddocks. The dams dried up, and the well was so low that the windmill no longer pumped water, so we dragged bucket after bucket of water up on a rope to fill the trough. We could not do it fast enough for the animals, though—they would drink it down before we had started on the next bucket. It was a long process.

Eventually, water had to be purchased by the truckload. Around the same time we were dragged off to church for special services put on for the farming communities to pray for rain. Being a teenager seemed a long, tiresome stint at times.

Naturally, a child would prefer being transported on a tractor through floodwater than having to spend their holidays eating peanut-butter sandwiches and drinking green cordial while on horseback, battling it out with the flies for their lunch. As a result, I have grown to absolutely adore the rain. Living in the tropics at one time was a dream come true, with heavy solid rain every day for months. I never tired of it. In fact, rain is one of the things in life I feel the most gratitude for.

You don't need to have lived through drought to appreciate rain, though. It is a gift to us all, a life force we need. Rain deserves gratitude, not criticism. We are blessed to have access to clean water. As Westerners, we have it very easy. Look at our fellow humans and how difficult a simple thing like a drink of clean, healthy water can be to obtain. People's whole lives revolve around the basics of survival, getting enough food and water to get through each day.

So before you complain about the rain again, or if you are looking to combat someone else's complaining, here are some points to consider.

Without rain:

1. We would be thirsty. Nothing we drink would exist without water.

2. We would be smelly. With no showers or water to swim in, we would get a tad rough on the nose before too long.

3. We would be very sunburned. No rain means trees don't grow; no trees mean no shelter. Even mud houses cannot be made without liquid.

4. There would be no flowers. What would a world be like without such beauty? I shudder to think of life without those kisses of color.

5. We would all be rather quiet. With nothing to drink, our mouths would dry up and produce no saliva. Conversations would surely cease if no liquid substitutes were possible.

6. We would be hungry. No rain means no veggies or other delicious healthy food. Or for the meat eaters, it means no crops to feed the animals, and no water for them to survive anyway.

7. We would have no excuse to stay at home unexpectedly. Rainy days give permission to do that for many.

8. We would be mighty unpleasant to the eye. As our bodies are mostly made up of water, if it were not replaced, we would shrivel up pretty fast—if we managed to live that long, which we wouldn't. But if we did, we would resemble prunes. Not that there would be any prunes to compare ourselves to. No rain, no prunes.

9. We would have no rainbows, one of the greatest losses of all. How can the sky show us its magical spectrum and restore our hope without water falling?

10. We would be dead, as simple as that, and within a very short time.

So let us rejoice on rainy days when everything is washed clean again. Let us treasure the sound of rain falling, and feel gratitude as we watch the natural world unfold as it has done for millions of years, long before we came along and started complaining about some clear, wet stuff falling from the sky.

The sun will shine again, so let us give thanks for rainy days. Let us focus on the blessings of rain, rather than the imagined inconvenience of it. It is a life force we cannot survive without. It is time to be grateful.

35

READY, SET, GO

It is a natural process for us humans to dream and want to expand our lives. Yet it has been said wisely by many that life is about the journey, not the destination. The destination, though, or the hope of it, is sometimes all that pulls you through the challenging times. But it is true—you must live in the now, as much as possible, to savor the gifts the present brings.

If hope is all that pulls you through, then hold on to that with all of your heart. Staying present, however, offers incredible peace, in that past wounds and conditioning or future fears don't hinder the moment. Although it may be a painful process to get to this place of presence within yourself, to break through the resistance of the old ways, the rewards are definitely worth it.

So how do you do both, live presently and work toward your dreams?

You enjoy the process of growing, giving gratitude for both the moment you are in and for where you will be. Prepare yourself for the life you imagine while still appreciating the day at hand. Then when the dream eventually arrives as a physical reality in your life, it is *already* a part of who you are.

It is not uncommon to be scared of actually attaining your dreams. The fear usually comes about by thinking too far ahead and worrying about how it will all happen and how it may change your life. But if you are able to maintain a sense of presence while working toward those goals, you will find that it is possible for each step to become gentle and clear, instead of tumultuous and frightening.

You don't just wake up one day and become ready for your dreams; you grow into them. And the only way to do this is to prepare yourself for the life you dream of and then grow into it, step-by-step. All of this makes dreams so much more attainable because you are bringing yourself closer to them all of the time, and life will reward your courage.

It is about faith and hope, certainly, but it is also about preparing yourself. It is about readiness. Work toward your dream, regardless of how many detours and roadblocks may challenge you along the way. Keep your vision clear yet flexible, as you may end up exceeding your initial vision through the many gifts of learning that you accumulate along the way.

None of this will be achieved, however, without the courage to begin. You must make a start, knowing that you are working toward your heart's desire, yet keeping your eyes open to the gift of life unfolding in the meantime. If you miss out on the present life in the chase, then you will *always* be chasing. You may achieve your goals but without fulfillment, as you are depending on the destination to complete you.

By trying to stay as present as possible, the mind is also infinitely clearer. Less energy is wasted in trying to control the outcome, which ultimately just blocks the flow anyway. A clear mind is more receptive to the sign-posts and opportunities along the way.

Life is certainly about now. But dreams are a natural accompaniment to the journey. So begin. Like a little child with a blank piece of paper to draw on, there will be a vision to work toward. It may turn out looking differently than initially imagined, but is that not a beautiful thing?

Work toward changing your ways, however that needs to be, regardless of how much this may challenge you—and it will. But just keep preparing yourself. Get ready for the life you desire. Make space for the dream to unfold in your life. Grow into it. It wants you, too.

Get yourself ready. Get yourself set. Before you know it, you are going. The momentum now supporting you has been building through all of your preparation over the years. And now life is rewarding your effort.

Instead of it being a frightening time where you hinder your success with fears by thinking too far ahead, you are able to be present and thoroughly enjoy your success, as you have already grown into it.

You are ready.

36

REMINDERS
FROM NATURE

A few weeks ago, a friend's dog gave me a great
reminder about persistence. My friend and I were hanging
out her washing as we chatted and caught up with each
other. All the while, her kelpie called Kevin (yes, Kevin
the Kelpie) dropped a stick at my feet. I'd throw it and off
he'd run to collect it. Within a flash he was back to do it
again, and again, and again. I really didn't mind, as I am
always an advocate for persistence and the rewards that
flow from such. So for most of my visit, including during
our cup of chai on her veranda, I continued to indulge
Kevin the Kelpie by throwing things for him.

The stick eventually became a splinter of almost
nothing. Then off he went and found a tennis ball. Obviously not every throw from me was particularly mindful,
as the ball finally came to land in a tree and stayed there.
A rest, I thought, relieved. But no, Kevin had other ideas.

He returned in a moment with the tiniest pebble, and on it went.

The game could have been over at any time I said so. Yet I admired his persistence, as I have had to develop similar qualities over the years as an artist carving her own path. Of course, there are ebbs and flows for anyone pursuing goals. Sometimes there are moments to persist and take quality action, and sometimes there are moments where you just have to let go and wait.

Being autumn, and getting closer to winter now, the days are shortening very quickly. With such a large mountain on the farm, the sun is already setting behind it by around 4:30 P.M. (until the solstice passes in a month or so, and the days begin to stretch out again). There is still more daylight left after 4:30, but with the sun gone, so has the warmth of its autumn rays.

Due to the angle of the planet at this time of year, though, those very last warm rays of the day shine directly onto me on the veranda. It is glorious and nurturing. Because of this angle, I am blessed with un-hindered rays of light. At other times of the year, the last rays of the day come through filtered trees—but right now, they are just magnificent, warming, direct rays.

This same golden light also shines onto the bugs that flitter about. It is amazing just how much life is actually going on in the world of flying insects that we don't usually see. With the sun as it is now, I can see them all. It is like when the sun catches the dust particles in the air through a window and they look like fairies, or small kisses of light. The enormous amount of insects in the world beyond this veranda is actually quite astounding.

As I have watched the abundance of life in the late afternoon sun, it has become obvious that these bugs were always flying about. Due to human eyesight not being as sharp as that of birds or some other animals, though, we usually don't see them. But that doesn't mean they are not there. They are. It just takes the right timing and angle (or perspective) to see them. When the light is right and the viewing perspective is also correct, a whole new world can be seen.

It is the same with our own lives and dreams. It all comes down to timing and the right perspective. When you are ready to see all that is already there, the light turns on and you can see it. It doesn't mean that it was never available before. It has always been there. It just takes you being in the right position in your life, with the right thinking, to reveal all that is waiting there and always has been.

It is an abundantly beautiful world. All that you need for your dreams to reveal themselves is persistence, like Kevin the Kelpie, followed by letting go at times, enabling you to see things from new angles.

Nature is a beautiful teacher. It so easily reinforces things you already know, but sometimes need to be reminded of. A dog with persistence, and an abundance of life usually blind to the eye, are wonderful reminders. Just because you cannot see something does not mean it is not there waiting for you.

The blessings are always there. You just need to look at life from a different angle sometimes.

37

RESPECT STARTS WITH OURSELVES

The heavy rains of the last two days have departed. Everything is washed clean, and the morning unfolds beautifully. Out my window I hear birds singing and the creek flowing. It is certainly not a bad way to spend a Monday morning.

I was chatting with a friend last night. She had been treated badly by some people and was looking within herself to try to figure out why. I explained how important self-respect is in how it affects the way we are treated by others. This was drawing on my own experiences and changes I had made at previous times, hence altering the way I was now treated and what I was willing to accept.

You can only be treated badly by people because it is either allowed or expected. The allowing is not usually done on a conscious level. Expecting it, though, may or may not be conscious. As long as you allow others to treat you disrespectfully, you will not be earning your own respect. When you break these patterns and earn your own respect, others treat you accordingly. You cease attracting such situations.

It is an unfortunate truth that most people do more to avoid pain than to give themselves pleasure. Instead of allowing the thoughts of pleasure to draw you forward, it is, more often than not, only the need to avoid any more pain that acts as the catalyst for change. Look at trying to lose weight, for example. As much as you dream of being healthier and want it so much in your heart, the success in changing only comes when the pain of being overweight becomes intolerable. Then the discipline and will to change your lifestyle carries you through. It is the same for anything—you do more to stop pain than to give yourself pleasure.

For many years I had someone close to me, someone I loved, using me as an excuse for their anger and dumping it on me every chance they could. I became the blame for anything and everything, and as a sensitive soul, I took a lot of it on, reacting in ways that only gave them more power. When the pain in my own life finally became too much, things changed. I spoke up, at last finding the courage to be completely honest. This ruffled feathers, and I was considered the worst person in the world for a long time. But I knew that the risk of losing this person from my life was worth it, as things could not go on as they were.

I was breaking patterns that had been in place for years, and this person did not like it. Despite them behaving in the same ways, they started to receive a different reaction. These reactions from me were honest and mature and no longer gave them any power. Years on, not only do I have their respect, but I have a loving relationship with them. Even more important, I have my own respect.

People will treat you as you allow them to. It doesn't matter if you know them well or not. You attract what you expect, on levels that often run very deep. By healing yourself and eventually improving your own self-worth, you then attract a life that supports your sense of who you now are, a life more worthy. When you reach this stage, you are then able to look at the anger or frustrations of others with detached compassion. It doesn't mean that you do not care. It only means that you are not willing to take it on anymore.

The best thing you can do toward earning the respect of others is to be honest and work toward respecting yourself, starting with being compassionate. Remember, you have to have compassion for your *own* humanness. None of us is perfect. If you can remember this, you can look at others *and* yourself compassionately. In turn, this will help everyone heal.

If you stumble and treat yourself in a way that is not respectful, acknowledge your humanness with loving compassion and just keep going. It is a gradual process, but when you earn your own respect this way, others will treat you well. If you continue working toward self-respect in a loving way, life will not deny you improved quality in your relationships. You will attract it naturally.

So if others are treating you in ways that are not suitable, look at your own expectations and see where this treatment is really coming from. You cannot save anyone else. You can only save yourself.

If you want to change the way others treat you, start by looking at how you treat yourself, emotionally as well as physically. Be compassionate. Be kind.

The rest will follow naturally.

38

SHEDDING
YOUR SKIN

Some children love school. Some just manage to get through it, longing to get home again. My own start to school was relatively peaceful, and overall, I did enjoy being a student and playing sports, along with the social connection that school offered.

The strongest memory of my earliest school years was from my first year in, and was not actually the happiest day. I recall being devastated to find out that plastic play money would not buy me a green drink from the school canteen. It was a heartbreaking discovery for a five-year-old optimist!

Show-and-tell was always fun, though, especially as I grew a little older and could search the farm for things to take to school. Sometimes it would be dead insects, or a weird piece of equipment from my father's shed, or some contraption that we children had created ourselves. I clearly remember bringing in a snake's skin one day, too, which ignited lots of great conversation between the teacher and the class.

While out walking down a country road recently, I came across another snake's skin. It not only reignited that happy childhood memory, but it also made me think about renewal and how I feel like I live in a new skin these days. I felt immediate gratitude and lightness.

As you go through life making conscious efforts to improve who you are, to discover your best self, you truly are creating a new version of you. The old self needs healing, but it is not necessary to carry your wounds forever. Yet sharing wounds with others can be addictive and an unconscious hindrance to moving forward. Discussing the emotional wounds you carry can bond you to others and ensure that you reach their kindest self through their pity of your story or through living with similar situations. Wounds can become your identity.

While there is certainly a time and need for expression of emotional pain, there does come a point when you are helping yourself more by moving on. Making a conscious effort about the words you speak is definitely an endeavor worth pursuing. Staying addicted to the story of your wounds can feel like a safe haven; it feels like a secure and familiar place. If you change, life changes, and that can be a terrifying thought. Life will change regardless, though, in one way or another. So isn't it better to be the driver of that change and its directions?

Write your fears out. Be honest with yourself. You can't lie to your own heart and to your cells. Your body knows. Your heart knows. Bring them relief through honesty. Why is changing into who you truly want to be scaring you? Through your answers, be open to discovering who you really are, with all of your wonder and beauty.

Moving forward and becoming the new version of yourself is frightening and challenging at times indeed. But being brave does not mean not being scared—it means that you are willing to move forward regardless, even if you *are* scared.

Trust in the big picture. Authenticity is a part of your soul's journey. You are here to discover who you really are, and then to share that wisdom with others. Bond with people over happy stories instead. Challenge yourself to go a week sharing only good stories and see how much lighter you feel.

There comes a time when you have no use for the old you anymore. Work through your healing, but then let it go. Embrace the new version of who you are. There is more joy and happiness in that life than you may yet dare to imagine.

There is a new you being born. It is time to shed your old skin.

39

SIGNPOSTS

Whenever I was new to another town or region, I always enjoyed getting to know the place by following my intuition and my own sense of direction. Sometimes I would get lost and sometimes I would find my way. Sometimes being lost led to other good things, too.

Even now, I still have this pattern of finding my own way around new places. I will use a map when I really have to, but not a minute before. Wandering around lost at times helps me discover areas I would not have, had I stuck to the main roads.

A GPS device will no doubt eventually work its way into my life one day, as technology does. But I'm in no rush for one. I would still prefer to ask local people for directions if I am lost. It adds an extra smile to my day, which often turns into a nice yarn with a stranger. Last time this happened, I ended up having a chat with an old guy in his driveway. The chat turned into such a lovely, friendly conversation that he invited me in.

Next thing I knew, he and his wife were proudly showing me through their home and pointing out the recent renovations they had done. I was there for over an hour. It was a beautiful moment in time. Not knowing my way turned out to be a lovely diversion, one that brought a very pleasant experience to both myself and the older couple.

Getting lost in places has often led me to wonderful discoveries. Linking streets and roads up is always a good revelation, too, as I get to know new towns and become more familiar with the back roads that the locals use. I enjoy those moments of realization, when a particular road leads to another that I may already know. Yet there are times when signposts are very handy, such as on long-distance trips. I love the ones that list a town almost a thousand kilometers away as if it were just up the road, close enough to have gained a mention on the sign with all of the other towns in between.

It isn't just roads for cars that have signposts, though. Life itself also tends to reveal some pretty obvious signs along the way. You can be focused on one particular direction and then a detour sign presents itself out of the blue, pointing you in a completely different direction. All of the signposts that previously pointed you one way disappear, and slowly but surely, new ones appear gradually, one at a time, toward a new direction.

Sometimes you can be cruising along well, and then a signpost sends you up a rocky road instead. You wonder how you didn't notice this change coming, how you could have been so blind to the other signs along the way leading to this. But even the things that block your intended way and send you off on another route bring their own gifts. Life is now seen from a new perspective, one that you wouldn't have considered had all the signs kept pointing down a straight and smooth road.

As you travel along the rocky road and have to use all of your energy to climb to the top of it, you reach a point where you can at last see beyond. The view is spectacular, offering you a whole different world to experience. You end up counting your blessings that the signposts pointed you this way after all.

Sometimes you can travel a road, and there are no obvious signs at all. That is when the need for your own intuitive signposts kicks in. You keep moving forward, not really knowing where you are going, only that life blocked the previous direction you were heading in.

It is at times like these that faith and trust are needed, along with the willingness to proceed a little bit at a time, trusting that the events unfolding are actually a beautiful thing. You just can't see the gifts this particular journey will bring yet. But you can't stand still for long either. Life continues to call you forward.

The past is gone. Forever. You can spend your time looking back at it, dwelling on what has been lost or what you could have done differently. Yet if you do, you are then missing today, the gifts it brings, and the signposts that are trying to lead you forward to a better future.

So you sigh and take one little step forward when you are brave enough to, doing what you can, one step at a time, listening to that quiet wise voice within. When you are not feeling so brave, you rest and wait for the next sign to reveal itself. And it does. It always does.

Not all signposts are obvious, though, and many of the best ones come in forms that do not necessarily appear pleasant. But if you dare to open your eyes and see where life is trying to lead you, the resistance lessens and the journey again becomes smoother and eventually joyous.

No one is immune from growth, learning, and the suffering that sometimes accompanies this. Yet there are always signs along the way to help. If you open yourself up to seeing them, and stay patient and trusting when you don't, it is definitely possible to create an easier life.

Of course, sometimes signposts don't always look like signposts. Sometimes they look like people who have caused a disruption in your life, the loss of some form of security you had, or nothing flowing properly for you. They can also come in the form of a passing comment, a synchronistic moment, a new person appearing in your life, or a memory coming to the surface that leads to you thinking about something current through a different perspective.

Whatever the signs are trying to tell you, trust them, and they will continue to become clearer. Keep your eyes and ears open. Look for the signposts. They are there waiting for you when you need them.

Just look for the signs.

40

STARTING AGAIN

I once read that at any given time, there is a fire somewhere on the planet. So if you look at the earth from a satellite, you will always find somewhere burning.

Overnight, more than 40 people lost their homes to recent fires on the outskirts of Perth, the capital city of Western Australia. A few years ago around the same time, 173 people lost their lives in bushfires in Victoria, and another 400 were injured. Complete towns were burned down, leaving nothing but cinders.

Those huge fires ripped through Victoria only two days before I was moving interstate. As a result, I came to see the decimation of the landscape as I drove through barren country of charred earth. Sheets of tin lay on the blackened ground—all that remained of some homes. Skeletons of trees stood alone on desolate hillsides.

At the time of those fires, North Queensland was suffering from major flooding. There was too much water in the north, and not enough in the south. Australia has had its share of extreme weather. Flash-flooding in towns of reasonable altitudes have killed people in recent years, as the walls of their homes suddenly gave way to the torrents passing through. Our third-largest city became a ghost town, almost apocalyptic, as floods rushed on through, not even noticing the man-made structures in its path, simply picking them up and taking them along. Many people were made homeless as a result.

A couple of years ago, the largest cyclone in Australia's recorded history arrived on the shores of North Queensland, decimating country towns, vast agricultural land and food supplies, and to my own personal sadness, a beautiful island that I once called home. My friends who were still living there not only lost their employment, but their homes, too.

Fires everywhere, including in South Australia and the Blue Mountains, have in the past taken plenty of homes and businesses in their wake. The same goes with recent floods in Victoria and Tasmania. And of course we see this all over the world, all of the time, on international news stories: floods and earthquakes in Asia, fires in America, floods and extreme cold in Europe, drought in Africa. On and on it goes . . . and it always will. Human life is subjected to the forces of nature. Natural disasters, as we call them, are actually a part of the earth's life and evolution. We will forever be reminded that at the end of the day, it is the earth that decides, not us.

So what do people do after such difficult times, when they have lost everything that gave them security— family members, homes, employment, food? They learn to receive. And they learn to start again.

Sometimes it is not natural disasters, but broken relationships, the loss of a loved one in death, or numerous other challenges that life can send. Either way, at some time in most of our lives, we all learn to start again in some capacity.

Some years back, after bushfires threatened towns on the outskirts of Sydney and roared through the surrounding bushland, my cousins and I went walking over the barren land. We were on our way to a waterhole for a swim. Every tree was charcoal. The earth was scorched bare. Rocks once hidden by vegetation were fully exposed. What struck me most, though, were the shoots of new life coming out of the trees and from the ground. Returning to the area near the waterhole again quite recently, a few years on, all I saw was healthy growth, a perfect picture of something that had survived the worst of it and come back even stronger.

Nature carries on after setbacks. It creates anew. As we are a part of this biological cycle, we too have the choice to start again, to renew, to carry on. Every single day gives us all an opportunity to start again, to commence brand new in one way or another, to begin once more.

So whether it is natural disasters, heartache, job loss, health challenges, or any other number of things that life can throw your way, you still have the choice to either give up or to start again.

It may take strength. It may take tears and frustration. But it may also bring fortitude and beauty you never knew you had inside of you.

It is a new day. It is time to start again.

41

THINGS TO CHEER YOU UP

Every one of us has bad days, and every one of us has good days. Both states pass. And both come again, in different ways.

Life is a balance of light and dark. Happiness comes not from being attached to the good days and dreading the bad days, but by accepting that both are a part of life. When you accept this, you are able to live from a more balanced perspective, with equanimity, enjoying the good times, learning from the hard times, and appreciating that both have a role.

There will never come a time when the learning stops. There is no point kidding yourself by saying when this or that happens, everything will be perfect forever. It won't be, because more learning will always come your way. It is when you accept this that life becomes easier. You become more equipped to cope with it and to understand. But there will always be learning.

Sometimes, though, the hard days linger longer. During these days, weeks, months, and even years, finding the strength to trust that the hard times will pass can be overwhelming. Hope may be all that draws you forward, and if you have been in a place of darkness for a long time, then even that is not always possible to draw upon.

So it is during such times that even the smallest steps are necessary to find some enjoyment in your day. Sometimes what is disguised as a little thing can be a huge catalyst in turning things around. When even finding a reason to get out of bed and get on with your day is a challenge, be gentle and kind to yourself and accept that perhaps right now, you are only capable of small steps.

Here are some little things you can do to feel better:

1. Buy some coloring-in pencils and draw, or buy a coloring-in book and color. It is very simple and childlike. But color carries many healing properties, and the distraction of drawing or coloring will bring you to a more present space, rather than dwelling on your situation. Anything creative with color will be beneficial.

2. Make a list of your best qualities—yes, you have some, everyone has goodness in them. Think of things you've done in the past, things that have left you feeling good. It may be what you've done, or it may be what you like about yourself. Maybe you once did a random act of kindness for someone, which no one else recognized needed doing. Or you like your smile, or that you used to be able to make people laugh (and you will again). Acknowledge these positive parts of yourself, without any reference to anything negative. No negativity allowed today.

3. Take yourself to somewhere with birds in their natural environment. Simply watch them go about their day. Listen to their joy in being alive, how they sing for the pure love of it. Watch the freedom of their flight. Birds have to survive and have their challenges, too, but they still remember to be joyous along the way.

4. Ban yourself from the computer for a whole day and night. Don't even turn it on. Have such days regularly. In the times we now live in, it is easy to forget about life going on outside. Computers are great in so many ways, particularly in the way they can bring people together. Yet in other ways, they can be very isolating. So turn yours off. Do something that you used to enjoy before the days of computers took over your life. Go for a walk. The exercise will be positive as well.

5. Call a friend who will make you laugh. Don't call someone who will wallow in your sadness with you, despite their kind intentions. Today is not a day for that. Just call a friend who will joke about nothing with you. If you cannot think of anyone, go for a walk in your neighborhood. Think of someone who serves you in your day-to-day life who is always cheery. Have a brief chat and laugh with them. They will enjoy it, too.

6. Dress in something that makes you look and feel nice, perhaps a brighter color than what you have been wearing. Pay attention to your appearance and take pride in yourself, no matter how much effort it takes. It doesn't matter if you think you are kidding yourself into feeling better. It is a change, and change is necessary to alter your current state. It is also an achievable goal when you are down.

7. Visit someone you know with children and hang out with the little ones for a while. Sing some songs, play make believe, hide-and-seek, anything. If there aren't any that you know nearby, just watch other children from a distance. Observe their simplicity and joy and remember that you too were once a child, and these qualities are still a part of you. Hop on a swing and lean back, get some wind beneath you, and feel yourself glide through the air.

8. Look through old photo albums and remember the happy times. Even if they bring memories that also make you sad, try to focus on the good times. It is easy to get caught up in feelings of loss, loneliness, or lack, rather than in the blessings that were once there. If there are no photos, think back to some fun memories and relive them in your mind. Laughing out loud is definitely permitted.

9. Eat healthy food. If you don't have the strength or energy to prepare something for yourself, go out and buy a fresh juice, a salad, or some soup. Chat with whoever serves you and smile at them. Healthy food heals both the body and the mind. So does smiling.

10. Have a beautiful bath. Use scents and candles. Make it a special thing, even if it is in the middle of the day. Nurture yourself. If you can, treat yourself to a massage; be pampered. Human touch is something we all need, and it is easy when you are down to isolate yourself, hence becoming touch starved. Hugs are always recommended, so hug someone if there is someone to hug. If not, go out and get some human contact, or pat an animal. We all need to be nurtured, and we all need touch.

Every little thing that you can do to change your current disposition will be far more beneficial than it may appear. Any glimpse of happiness or hope, no matter how small, is better than none at all.

If you manage to do just one of these things, then congratulate yourself for the effort. It doesn't matter if you are not strong enough to be the person you once were. Trust that healing is happening in your life now. You don't have to become who you were; rather, you will become who you are meant to be when this healing time has passed. It will be someone new, someone amazing, someone accepting, someone happy.

It may not feel like you will smile again, but never lose hope. You *will* smile again. You simply will. And that in itself is worth smiling about, is it not?

42

THIRTY SECONDS

It was a regular peaceful night a couple of weeks ago, when things changed unexpectedly. A rumbling began that sounded like a truck driving very close to the house. Mirrors shook, and birds screeched in the night. After about 15 seconds it stopped, only to be followed very soon after by another rumbling. This time there was no mistaking it as a truck. It was our living planet, Mother Earth, reminding us that like everyone and everything, she is forever changing. It was the tremor of the earth, quaking 17 kilometers below the surface—its center under a lake, about an hour's drive away.

Thirty seconds of rumbling. No warning. No time to make changes in one's life. Thirty seconds that could have, effectively, been the last thirty seconds of many of our lives. We then waited for another rumble, but all was still and remained that way.

We were spared any injury or damage, and thank-fully, there were no injuries reported throughout the region. But it was a great reminder of how quickly life can and does change.

Had the quake been any bigger, we may have been running for our lives, with roofs collapsing or walls falling in. It sounds dramatic, and even though it was only a smaller quake, for those who know larger quakes, it *was* dramatic. Plenty of people have lost their lives in earthquakes and other unexpected events without even 30 seconds' notice.

With 30 seconds, though, there is space for thought and even a small slice of reflection. Of course, in that time frame, had the quake been large enough to cause immediate structural damage, there would have been no time to grab anything but my daughter and get outside. It brings home how irrelevant belongings are when it truly comes to the crunch. With no time to spare, the only thing that matters are loved ones.

Like many people, I have had friends who died suddenly in collisions. Thirty seconds would have been a long time to them, but they were not given even that. Obviously, many people are given a longer period for reflection, like the people I used to care for (and wrote about in my memoir). Some are given no time at all; some are given 30 seconds.

I was thinking about this short gift of time in the brief moments between the two quakes. We don't live in an area known at all for earthquakes. The last slight tremor was recorded 43 years ago. This one, like the last, came out of nowhere, a clear reminder yet again that we are never completely in control.

You never know when it is your last 30 seconds. You truly don't. But if you were given that brief bit of time, what thoughts would pass through your mind? For me, and for most I am sure, it was loved ones and little else.

It is so easy to focus on the details of day-to-day living. We live in a world full of details. But when all else falls away, the importance of the things trying to rob most of our attention disappears and we are reminded of what is truly important in life. *Love.*

Sometimes reminders come out of the blue, like the rumbling of the earth beneath us. Yet these reminders of how quickly life can end are really just blessed wake-up calls.

If your life were to end today, how would you like to spend your last 30 seconds? Is the direction of your current life already aligned with that?

If not, it is time for change.

43

THOUGHTS
AND TRAFFIC

The other day I was sitting in the shade of a lovely tree, watching the traffic go by as I waited for an appointment. Cars pulled up at the traffic lights, far enough away for privacy, but close enough that I could see many of the faces waiting for the green light.

An old man was waiting patiently in the traffic. He looked quite dignified, especially when compared to some of the tradesmen in other vehicles nearby. I guessed him to be in his late 80s and wondered what changes he had seen in his lifetime. His car was a very modern little thing. I thought about his potential childhood and how *any* car would have been a big deal back then. *What did his first car look like compared to the one he now drives?* I wondered.

Even in my own time, I have seen so many changes. I watched Ernie and Bert from *Sesame Street* go from black and white to color (which was pretty amazing as a kid), then from puppets to digital. I have watched vegetarianism become mainstream, thank goodness. Banks have given up valuing loyal customers and now charge for the luxury of even providing a bank account. Seat belts have become compulsory. Smoking has been banned indoors in many places. Fax machines have arrived, as have computers, the Internet, mobile phones, fast cars, fast living, and so many other things. Even handwritten Christmas cards are almost extinct, giving way to group e-mails or electronic cards.

So, I pondered, what must a man of almost 90 have seen in his lifetime? Yet here he was, adjusting to life in modern times, going with the flow, waiting patiently at the traffic lights, and still driving himself to town, with independence.

In the next flow of traffic halted at the same light, I observed a young guy who was incredibly impatient, growing more and more agitated waiting for the light to change, his music blaring out the windows all the while. When the light did change, he almost ended up in the backseat of the car in front of him due to such impatience. I wondered about his story and what could genuinely be so important to create such angst within him. I felt sorry for him, really. So much learning still to do. When he could, he managed to change lanes and overtake most of the other cars, only to find himself waiting at yet another set of lights. I wondered what he would see in his lifetime, and at what point he may slow down enough to notice.

Every day there are opportunities to people watch, and in doing so, many unexpected lessons can be presented to us, due to the relaxed state and floating thoughts. In the 20 or so minutes that I sat under that tree, I marveled at many lovely aspects of humanity.

I saw a young mum singing to her child, who was about four years old. She was also pushing a stroller with two younger children in it, one a toddler and one a babe. It was a weight to push, and the day was getting very hot (hence my sitting in the shade in the first place). Yet here she was, singing and happy with her three children, getting on with her day walking up an incline while impatient drivers sat in traffic nearby. Attitude makes such a difference!

I wondered about the stories of all who passed me as I sat under that tree and thought about how many books or movies could be created simply from the lives of the people passing by that one little intersection. This led my thoughts to the beauty of humanity again, with compassion for who we are as a species. We have made so many mistakes and definitely need each other's compassion (and our own). Yet we are all beautiful in our humanness, trying to get on with our lives in the mad societies we have created as a whole. I just hope that as a species, we continue to make the necessary changes for the survival and happiness of ourselves and of our magnificent planet.

Everyone has a story, and none of us can know the whole of another's story. But there is goodness in everyone, even those who have not yet tapped into it in themselves, those who show only their unpleasantness. Even they have goodness within.

Taking the time to people watch is a wonderful thing, even more so when the opportunity presents itself unexpectedly. And if you see someone watching you, then consider that, just perhaps, you have inspired them to have some unexpected insight, simply for the un-conscious role you may have played in their day.

We are all more connected than we realize. We have more in common than we realize. And, especially, we are all far more beautiful than we will ever realize.

44

THREE SOPRANOS

The willow tree is full of leaves again, and spring is fast turning into summer. This week walking has been limited to before seven in the morning, as the heat of the day arrives soon after. Ocean and river swims are starting to beckon instead.

With the unfolding of the spring season comes new birth. My favorite bird around here, as previously mentioned, is a particular willy-wagtail. While in Aboriginal folklore the bird is considered a stealer of secrets, I do trust this one and enjoy our friendship immensely.

Her nest this season was built on a railing in the carport, with my van receiving a dollop of bird droppings daily for a short time. But patience was warranted and rewarded well when three little heads peered out over the top a couple of weeks ago.

Their growth from this moment was phenomenal. Two days after their heads reached the top of the nest, they were struggling to fit in there and were standing on each other. The following evening, I was in my usual spot on the veranda to enjoy the sunset, and I saw that all three were on a railing near their nest but no longer in it. I marveled at them in delight. It was their first outing from the nest, and I was there to see it.

The following morning, I was surprised to not even have to go the carport. All three were on the fence in front of the cottage. Their first day of flying had happened, and like a proud mother, I stood and watched them in joy. Since then I have watched them in the trees down near the creek. They also hang around the veranda a decent amount, too. As their mother trusts me, they have learned to do the same.

Willy-wagtails have two sounds: One is like talking; it sort of sounds like *ch-ch-ch*. The other is singing. It uses the talking when threatening other birds. They are highly territorial and will harass birds much bigger than themselves (kookaburras, for example). But they also use it when talking to each other. Then there is their song.

For the first week and a half, the babes didn't sing. They would fly along in front of me when I walked, but with no singing. Then a couple of days ago it happened. I heard them sing.

I was delighted to see that they enjoyed their vocal discovery as much as I did, so much so that they couldn't stop singing once they started. Hearing one of the babes start its singing at 3:30 the following morning, even beating the kookaburras who are always the earliest risers, brought a smile to my face in the midst of sleep. Its solitary song of joy rang out through the night, accompanied only by frogs, who were busy singing their own delightful tunes by the creek.

This morning the whole family of willy-wagtails came to visit. They blessed the cottage and its surroundings with an orchestra of perfect harmonies, as they sang and sang. It was joyous.

There are three new singers in the world now, and that is a wonderful thing—three more songs to be heard, three more singers adding to the world's existing chorus. It is like having my own version of the Three Tenors, although they're definitely not tenors. I should call them the Three Sopranos. Yes, very fitting, the Three Sopranos and Their Fluffy Feathers.

Unless you are blessed with being able to live in nature almost completely, you may not even know that some of the birds you hear are singing for the very first time in their lives. But every bird has to have a first song.

So if it is spring in your world, do consider that you may be hearing an absolutely brand-new tune. If it isn't spring yet, please keep this in mind when it does come around. Many of the birds that look like all of the others of their breed may in fact only be a few weeks old and are breaking into their very first song ever. Whatever songs they're singing to you, though, will be joyous.

Life is enjoyed so much more when you allow yourself to stop sometimes and just *listen*.

45

TIMING

In the early 1990s, I lived and worked on a tropical island for a couple of years. It truly was one of the most beautiful places imaginable. Rain forest covered the mountain and valleys. Coral reefs surrounded it, with the main sections of the Great Barrier Reef only a short boat trip out. Wildlife was abundant. Fun was aplenty.

The main way to get to the island, if you didn't have your own boat, was by water taxi. A family-run business on the mainland transported staff, resort guests, and day-trippers back and forth several times per day. All times on the schedule were given in "North Queensland time," meaning that they were never exact.

This was hot, humid country, and things were done slower here. It took time to unload people and baggage. Sometimes it worked efficiently, sometimes not. As a relatively punctual person, this was a great lesson for me in surrender and learning to just go with the flow. It also gave me more coping skills for life when I finally returned to live on the mainland. I had not been particularly rigid prior, but I certainly left the island being much more relaxed, about everything.

A habit that many in the busy modern world form is to run everything by a clock, often down to the minute, but life doesn't actually work that way. Not the big picture of life, anyway. Time is a man-made institution, separating the light and dark of the planet's natural turning into units of hours, days, weeks, and so on. This enables the human race to function, or try to, with some control.

Life works with its own schedule, though, and the more you can let go and trust this, the more you actually allow things to flow. If you are living on faith, you come to realize that things will come when you need them, rarely before. It is only fear that dictates they must fall into place sooner.

What you need *does* come, if it is not blocked by fear or terror. You can try to bargain with life and control every step, but in order to live with courage that allows for miracles, you need to learn that things will happen in God's time, not yours. And when they do, they will be perfect, despite any fears that may try to contradict that idea in the meantime.

At the "last" minute, money can come to you from seemingly nowhere. The contact you need will arrive in your life at the perfect moment. A vehicle will turn up from a source you had never imagined. Miracles such as these happen every day—they always have and they continue to. Even as you are reading this, a miracle is unfolding somewhere for someone right now.

During the lead-up to my giving birth to my daughter, my work took flight and gained great momentum. It had been 14 years of focus, determination, and hard work to raise it to this level. When it took off, though, there was no holding back its impetus. The previous year

or two had indicated that my work was gaining a wider audience, and I grew into that comfortably, as I was ready. However, I didn't imagine the enormity of pressure that would come when it made news in some of the world's leading newspapers.

About three weeks before my daughter was born, I was looking at Hay House Australia's website, wondering when they were going to offer me a contract. I had published independently within a division of the company, solely with the intention of Hay House noticing me. It was my dream to be published by them, as I wanted to do conscious, ethical business, not just business. Things were getting busier and busier, and I wanted and needed help, in order to maintain some balance.

The momentum continued and then exploded about the time I was due to become a mother. Instead of lying on the hospital bed in labor, enjoying the incredibly special event that was about to unfold, I was doing interviews on my mobile phone and fending off more media, all while my body was having contractions.

At around midnight, I eventually turned off my phone and closed the computer, allowing me to properly savor the blessing of what was happening. As I lay in the semi-darkness of the hospital room, I sent out a prayer for help in the business part of my life. Instead of enjoying its success, I felt sadness. It was robbing me of being more present with what was even more important to me—my baby. I wanted to be a mother first and foremost. I needed time for that and longed to hand over the reins of my work.

In the morning, I gave birth to my darling daughter. The overwhelming rush of love I felt for her as we first looked into each other's eyes made the rest of the world fall away from my consciousness. Nothing else mattered.

I didn't turn the computer on at all that day. But when I turned my phone on to share the news with loved ones, more media pressure was waiting. So I turned the phone back off after making my personal calls, and trusted that somehow I would find a way through it all. I felt gratitude now for the success, but renewed determination not to allow it to ruin this time in motherhood.

The morning after, I was still in hospital, in my night-dress with my one-day-old little girl beside me. Exhaustion from the previous day and from my first night with her (and the reality of what no sleep was truly going to mean) overwhelmed me. Then out of seemingly nowhere, my phone rang. I answered it to hear a cheerful, wonderful voice introducing himself as the Managing Director of Hay House Australia. And right there and then, he offered me an international publishing contract. Beautiful!

Yes, timing is indeed a wonderful thing. Never underestimate that what you need is not already on its way to you. It arrives in God's time, though, not necessarily at a time you dictate. This wonderful divine source sees the big picture and understands timing in ways that humans may never.

If you are genuinely going to live a life true to yourself, leave room for miracles. It will take faith and a certain amount of surrender, learning to trust in the perfection of divine timing. Yet in doing so, you will create the life your heart dreams of. Then when you look back at the end of your time on earth, you will know peace, for you will have lived authentically, with bravery and faith.

Trust in timing. It is more perfect than you know.

46

VARIETY
AND COLOR

My favorite color was always purple. I was in love with it for ages. For a few years in a row, some of us who had birthdays near each other even celebrated with "Purple Passion Parties," all of which included purple cakes, purple punch, purple desserts, and, of course, people dressed in purple. I still love purple, but am not sure if it's my favorite. There isn't one color in particular that is my favorite these days. I love them all!

I chose four colors for the inside of our home. An interior-designer friend told me that if you have a view, it looks great to paint that wall darker to frame the scene. So while the living areas are a happy but not over-the-top yellow, the front wall that frames the mountains is a deep crimson. It works beautifully, despite my thinking it was going to be more of an eggplant/aubergine color initially. When it hit the walls, I was surprised by the difference of tone from the sample card. It didn't matter, though. I adjusted.

Regardless of whether the colors turned out as expected or not, they change due to the angles of light at various times of the day anyway. So they were never going to be *exactly* as I had anticipated.

The same thing happens with the light and angles we view our own lives by.

When things are starting to move forward, gaining momentum, you are feeling your way into your new life. It starts to become more natural and comfortable. Changes in your physical life also continue to flow. This is because the effort and focus applied previously is now affecting your subconscious mind, the part of yourself that actually attracts things to you.

The subconscious mind has been programmed since birth, so there will be old patterns that occasionally surface. A seemingly bad day may arise amongst some forward flow, but it doesn't need to be interpreted as a huge disaster. It is simply a bump in the road. The old mind may want to create a drama of it, leaving you feeling like you haven't progressed at all, but you have. Use contrast in a positive way. It is an essential part of life and helps you define what is most important to you and most desired.

Keeping a journal or even looking back on photos is an encouraging way to remind yourself of how far you have actually come. On challenging days, rather than succumb to old self-defeating thought patterns, give yourself encouragement. Acknowledge that you are doing really well. You are trying to make changes. You are putting in the effort. You are becoming the person you want to be. Believe me, life rewards effort. So the sooner you can knock those old self-defeating thoughts out of the way, the sooner you will move forward in yourself again.

It takes conscious choice as to what angles you view your life from. Those conscious choices then reshape the unconscious, one thought at a time, one moment at a time, one day at a time. The subconscious mind will believe whatever you feed it with. So feed it well with encouragement and self-love, knowing that you *are* progressing. Don't lose sight of your intentions and the life you are truly here to live. Bumps in the road need only be that, nothing more. The subconscious will continue to attract what you focus on, so focus on the positive changes and continue to feel your way into your dream.

There will be bumps and diversions. They do not need to be interpreted as the end of the world or the end of your dream, because they are not. And while you may not be seeing things at the perfect angle or shade that you hoped, perhaps a slightly different angle or shade is not such a bad thing. Your willingness to accept some slight variations of your vision may actually turn out far better in the long run. Always trust that there is wisdom to be found through challenges. You are still moving in the right direction.

So if your day starts out with some shades of color you don't really want to see, trust that you are capable of viewing things differently at another time, in the same day. There is a positive to be found in any situation. What you choose to focus on, what you choose to feed your subconscious with, and what you therefore choose to attract is up to you and the angles you view life from.

Allow your life to be a colorful celebration. There are so many fantastic shades to be found. It only takes opening your eyes to the beauty.

47

WHAT, NOT HOW

After a few days away, the return to the farm showed that heavy rains had fallen. The drive in was slippery, the grass alongside the route waterlogged, and the creek was overflowing. Of course I love the creek flowing this much, as it can then be heard through the bedroom window in the quiet of night.

This sometimes means that the van must be parked on the other side of the creek, in case the water rises more, hiding the rickety bridge almost completely. It is rare, though, and worth the trudge across in gum boots. Country life is beautiful in so many regards. So having to work with nature at such times is no problem at all.

The force of nature is indeed the ruler. We only need to see the huge effects of changing weather patterns to confirm this. But by "nature," I don't just mean trees and ocean. To me, nature is God, the universe, Dhamma, and any other name you wish to give to the Great Spirit that resides within and around us all.

So while there are human, animal, and plant lives lost through various forces of nature—such as changing weather patterns, earthquakes, tsunamis, and numerous other incidents—there are human, animal, and plant lives blessed by nature's powerful forces as well. It is good to also remember that, each and every day, life blesses many people with prayers answered through unexpected channels.

You do what you can to create the life you dream of. You work toward your goals. You take what action you can. You put your prayers and intentions out there, along with your gratitude. Constantly learning to then let go and trust that what you need will come to you in its own way is one of the hardest things to remember and implement on a regular basis, at least until it becomes habit.

Yet at the end of the day, *how* things come to you is up to God. Thankfully, the creative abilities of the universe are phenomenal. Most people block the flow by spending too much time focusing on the "how" rather than the "what." Trusting in the wisdom of the universe makes life a much more joyful process, not to mention simpler.

It is easy to get caught up in taking things too seriously at times. Life can be a beautiful and joyous process, though, when you allow it to be—one worth rejoicing for.

A bird out my window agrees, as its delightful song floats on the sunshine into my office. It is singing for the pure joy of being alive. It understands that the *how* of things is not important. That's God's job, and one that is done perfectly.

How blessed we all are, especially when we remember to let go and let God.

48

WISHES IN
THE WIND

I don't know where the myth or idea came from that if we make a wish while blowing dandelions into the wind, our wish will come true. But as a result, fuzzy flowers were blown to the wind in high numbers during my childhood, and probably yours as well.

Being an adult hasn't changed things that much for me. I still send my wishes on dandelions sometimes. It is fun to send desires to the wind. Sometimes what you wish for, though, are just temporary longings or playful wishes. And sometimes your whole heart can be in it, sent with a prayer of genuine yearning.

Some folks feel that they must have this or that to be happy, as they blow their wishes to the wind. A prime example of this came from a friend of mine some years ago. She told me that she would finally be happy if she only owned some nice jewelry. Having gold hanging off her wrists and neck was the catalyst needed for her happiness, apparently. I laughed with her, despite her sincerity. Thankfully, life threw enough lessons her way to see her shifting her priorities significantly over the years. She is a much happier person these days (and she still doesn't own much jewelry).

Of course happiness comes before all of that. Rather than depend on events falling into place or things coming your way before you can be happy, it is when you find happiness within, regardless of outer circumstances, that things then flow your way.

I was chatting with an older friend recently about the delightful twists and turns life can throw us, even if often not enjoyable at the time, and he laughed with enthusiasm. "Yes!" he said. "Thank God I didn't get everything I wished for in my life. Thank God!'" Looking back, he could see how much more interesting and satisfying his life became when he let go of the need to control the outcome. When his exact wishes weren't met, life had better surprises in store for him.

By embracing the lessons and surrendering with trust that whatever is happening is for your best, life flows more naturally and generously to you. Blowing your wishes to the wind is symbolic, too, and rituals do put energy into motion.

Now, sometimes the wishes will arrive in a different format or appearance than what you had imagined. But they are still your wishes granted. They will still bring your heart the feelings it is longing for, and more. It is your wish answered. But will you see it?

Often people don't recognize when a wish has been granted, because they are trying so hard to control the exact outcome. That need to control and say, "I want things *exactly* this way or that way," only brings pain, resistance, and heartache, all of which are unnecessary. All that is needed is to surrender and trust. It takes strength at times, but it truly is all that you need.

So next time you blow a dandelion to the wind with your wish, allow that wish to find its own way back in its own time. Allow it to reveal itself in its own perfect way. And sooner or later you will find yourself delighted that it came in the form it did, not in the form you had originally wished for.

Your wishes are heard and, in their own time, they will unfold.

49

WONDER OF
THE BODY

Throughout the years, I have experienced constant reminders of just how intelligent the body's own healing system is. One only has to witness how quickly a body goes into repair mode, from a simple cut on the hand to expelling food that does not agree with it. The body *wants* to heal itself. Sometimes it can do it alone, and sometimes it needs a combined effort from you.

My own body has been an amazing friend to me. I have come to understand just how clearly it communicates in order to keep both my physical and emotional health balanced and functioning at its best. As a loyal friend, I do what I can to honor the wisdom and advice it gives me on a regular basis. I also look for the blessings and learning being offered when I am experiencing illness, and work with it as I am guided through my healing.

As is the case with everyone, each body is different and responds to different needs and lifestyles. Twenty-five years ago, I realized that eating meat did not suit my body (or my philosophies). Ten years later, I took a couple of months off eating dairy products as well, and realized just how much the vegan lifestyle assisted the smooth functioning of my body. I've never looked back.

I am not sure if such a lifestyle suits everyone's body or not. That is what makes us all so individual and wonderfully unique. You have the right to listen to your own body and to adhere to the advice it gives. I have come to understand the needs of mine and constantly listen to it. Things do change along the way, of course, as the body continues its own evolution.

The greatest honor you can give to your health is to listen to your body and apply the advice it gives. Many of the people I cared for during my years in palliative care said how they wished they had listened more to their bodies. It is easy to ignore the signs of illness, at least initially. Yet the body communicates from a loving place, and if you don't listen, there is no guarantee that your health will continue to keep you company.

The time to die will come to us all. Staying healthy and treating your body with the respect it deserves is not about denying your inevitable death. It is about maintaining the best quality of life while it is your turn to be living. You have free will in how you treat yourself— choosing positively provides a personal reward of health and independence.

The freedom to decide one's own path to healing is also given to us all. Just as you can choose your religion, philosophies, and lifestyle, you find your own way to the lessons and wisdom you are here to discover. You may read various books that appear to come from completely different angles, but when you get to the bottom of it, truth is truth. When you resonate with that, you know you have found the right book or path for your own healing.

A disease may be relatively common and affect many people, but the path to healing that disease is an individual choice. Either way there are always blessings being offered, even when the body communicates to you through this form. All illness presents the opportunity for emotional healing, too, often with the body catching up once the heart and mind have significantly healed.

The body and its natural operating systems are truly remarkable creations. When you stop to think about everything that is happening within you on a minute–to-minute or day-to-day basis, it can be overwhelming, but in the best possible way.

As my lungs go on breathing and passing oxygen to all of my body, without me even asking it to, and my ears listen to the birds singing all around me, I thank my body for being the amazing intelligent creation that it is.

How blessed we are by the splendor of who we are! Isn't that worth looking after?

50

WORDS WE SPEAK

I always find nature to be the best teacher of all. Every day I see things unfolding in the natural world that offer teachings to us in the human world. (Of course the human world is a part of the natural world, too, but we have lost sight of that somewhat.)

Driving along, I saw a small bird injured on the road. As cars passed by, a larger bird kept returning to pick at the smaller one, which was clearly dying but not quite there. Unfortunately, there was traffic behind me so I couldn't stop, but I was relieved to see that on my way back ten minutes later, the little bird had indeed died, so it no longer had to suffer being picked at anymore.

It reminded me of another occasion, a similar scenario. A friend had just arrived from England, and we were in Brisbane, showing her around. We then spotted a mother duck with about eight ducklings waddling along behind her. As we all cooed about how beautiful the scene was, a huge black crow swooped down and collected the last little duckling in its claws and flew off. (You can imagine the change of expression on our faces.)

How often, though, do we as humans do something comparable? The strongest of the species regularly attacks the weaker. It may not be in an act of cannibalism, but verbally and emotionally instead. It just doesn't make sense.

If you've read my memoir, you know that most of my first few decades were spent having verbal cruelty and criticism aimed at me. But just as the bullied can become the bully, I learned to criticize others. After all, it was a skill I had been taught over and over for far too long. My natural manner was actually to build people up, to inspire them—but in particular relationships, my long-established patterns instead caused me to sometimes fall into the habit of criticizing others.

Thankfully, there came a point when I made a very conscious decision to either end those relationships or to advise the people that I was no longer willing to add any more of that energy to the world. It was a clear decision, a moment I can recall easily, and from that point on, I chose to speak more consciously.

I am pleased to say that the habit is long past. Not only do I not criticize anyone, but I no longer have such relationships in my life with others who criticize. I am also detached enough from criticism now that any directed at me from strangers or others, as will happen when a part of your life is in the public eye, is nothing more to me than a lesson in compassion.

Having made such a conscious decision, though, and having broken any old habits in this regard, I seem to have developed a new alertness to criticism by people to others. And I am still amazed by how much energy is given in our society to condemning each other. Just like the bird on the road, with that pointed beak picking and picking, the human mouth is also capable of causing immense pain.

We all have strengths and we all have weaknesses. A conscious decision to change verbal patterns, however, benefits everyone. None of us is perfect, and the sooner we give each other a break by watching what words we speak, the sooner our own lives improve, as well as those around us.

So, do you want to be the bird picking at the other when it is down, so much so that it just longs for it all to be over? Or would you prefer to be like the bird that flies happily and freely above, bringing pleasure to all who hear the joyful sounds that it shares?

I know which I choose.

Kindness can go a long way.

51

WORKING TOGETHER

Whether you are living a life of solitude or one in which you don't have a moment to yourself, it is healthy to remember that there are a lot of people out there on the same wavelength, people living from their hearts and wanting a better world for everyone, too. Even though there may be times that you feel totally alone and misunderstood in the world (and we have all felt that way at some time), it is comforting to remember that whether you know them in your everyday life or not, there are still kindred souls out there wishing you happiness.

You have skills to share. We all do. You are needed in this positive equation as much as everyone else. But you also need support systems. Sometimes these are obvious systems, like friends or families. Sometimes they consist of people who share similar habits, like a sports club helping you to achieve your goals. Sometimes, though, it is not so obvious, and you may feel like you are doing things totally alone.

Yet no achievement is ever accomplished completely alone. Often the pieces of the puzzle are in place years in advance, without you having any idea of the relevance a particular person, job, or situation is going to play in bringing things together at a future time. Later, when you look back and see all of those links, you realize just how many people are actually in your support system, whether you knew it or not. Sometimes they don't even know it consciously. Yet they can play a major role, simply by doing something that they've given very little thought to afterward. Or perhaps it is the other way around: you are playing a vital role in someone else's support system, without yet being completely aware of it.

So I ask that as you read this, please send some goodwill out there to all of those who are trying to improve their lives, to all who are working toward happiness. Send goodwill also to everyone who offers their smile to the general public through their work, and to the other people who will read these same stories, in different locations around the world. Just by having that awareness, you are already generating more goodwill in the world and in each other's lives.

Nothing good can be achieved alone. We must work together, and even a heartfelt intention to send kindness helps enormously. If you are seeking support yourself, just trust that it is out there and working its way to you—but you do have to open up to it.

Allowing others to help you may be a hard lesson. By learning to receive, though, you allow them the pleasure of giving. If you remain closed to receiving, you not only block the flow of help to you, but you deny others that pleasure of giving. As anyone who is a giver knows, it is a pleasure to do so. Yet it is often the givers who are the worst at receiving.

Sometimes you are the giver and sometimes you have to be the receiver. Be open to working together on all levels, to allow the flow of give-and-take to weave its balance around the world. Give some good wishes. Receive some good wishes. Give a helping hand. Receive a helping hand. No one can truly do it all alone, and at some time, we all learn to do both. It keeps things balanced.

As anyone who has ever felt unbalanced knows, maintaining balance is a healthy way to live. Let us work together. Let us remember our connectedness. Let us be the best we can be. Let us unite.

52

WORRY NO MORE

As I sit at my desk and look out, it is the distant mountains that usually draw my eyes to them. Between my desk and those mountains, though, is a valley—and closer still, our yard, and the trees that make it what it is. One of these is a mulberry tree, and being winter, it currently stands bare. Yet come springtime, the tree will be lush with foliage, followed by an abundance of juicy purple fruit.

Once again, nature indicates how cyclical life is. We humans are natural beings, too, who create happiness best when learning to flow with the seasons of our lives.

There will be loss, but there will be love. There will be barren times, when it feels like nothing is flowing your way, but there will also be abundant times, where blessings fall at your feet. There will be tears, but there will be laughter. There will be times of immense stretching, but there will be times of enjoyable rest. There will be questions, but there will be answers. There will be surrender, but there will be hope.

The life you choose to experience is up to you. Your thoughts, words, and actions are creating your tomorrows right now. Whether you choose to maintain consciousness of this or not is your decision. It makes no difference in regard to how it works. The energy created by your thoughts and words attract matching situations in your physical life, no question about that. You are definitely creating your own life. Living consciously or not, however, makes a huge difference in whether it will be a life that you will look back on peacefully or with regret.

It is time to give yourself permission to be you, to be the *authentic* you, the person who has been waiting underneath all of the conditioning of your past, underneath the pain and growth, underneath it all. It is time to be you. The starting point for this is creating the habit of making more conscious, loving choices.

Sure, life will challenge you, stretch you, and test you to see how strong you truly can be. But life will reward you, too. Every effort, or lack thereof, generates a physical manifestation. Plant the right seeds. Be gentle, be patient, but plant the right seeds—for you.

Allow others to also be who they are trying to be. Put your judgment in the rubbish bin and send it on its way. Acceptance and a sense of belonging contribute enormously to good health and true happiness. So allow others to be themselves, and watch them bloom before your eyes.

Mostly, though, allow yourself to be you. If you do not yet know who that is—if the flame of that amazing, beautiful person is only just starting to be felt—then ask, "Who am I truly here to be?" Ask this over and over. The flame of your authentic self has never been extinguished but will begin burning brighter, shedding light on your question, one layer at a time. You are allowed to be wonderful and amazing (and you *are*). Live the life your heart wants. It is safe to be you. Give yourself permission and be grateful, especially for that freedom of choice.

The mulberry tree does not worry every winter when its leaves have left it exposed to the world, when the birds that keep it company in warmer months are nowhere to be seen. It simply rests and waits, preparing itself for another season of immense growth, knowing that springtime will come again. It understands that there are seasons, with time for rest and time for growth.

So worry no more. Make positive, self-loving, conscious choices. Do not give negative people your power. Feel compassion for them, but continue to build your tribe of positive, accepting people. Treasure yourself. Be real. Share your light. And above all, let yourself *laugh!*

Know that despite your humanness and any challenge that may test you, you are consciously creating a better life, one you are proud of, one that will add goodness to the lives of others and yourself, and one that will free you completely from the experience of regret.

You are allowed to be happy. You are allowed to be joyous.

It is time.

AFTERWORD

No Regrets

Life is about learning. There is no doubt about that. It is about learning to love, learning to let go, and learning to live in the kindest way toward ourselves and others. Many think it is about money, power, achievement, and ownership. But even those people work it out, given time for reflection at the end.

Of course even now, it is easy to look back on your life and think of the things you would do differently, given your time again. The human life is not one of consistency and perfection, though—it is one of flux. Within it is happiness and sadness, learning and loss. Therein lies its actual perfection, in its imperfection. Everything you learn is a part of your journey and a gift in itself.

Rather than looking back with regret for the things you would do differently, you can choose to accept your humanness and imperfection. This is a much more gentle way to approach life.

As for me, I would have treated my body with more kindness and respect when I was younger. I would have spoken up more often in my own defense, rather than expose myself to years of verbal and mental abuse from others. I would have also been kinder in response.

I would have taken even more risks. I would have looked in the mirror and said "I love you" years before I actually did. I would have said "Thank you" to life more often. I would have done a lot of things differently. But I didn't, because I am human.

So I look at who I was and I love her anyway. She was frail, broken, conditioned. She was *human,* and for that, I can give her compassion. In doing so, there is no place for regret. There is only love and kindness. Regret is a very harsh judgment and not necessary if you are able to come from a place intended for self-love.

Look back on who you were as compared to who you are now, and love the person you see, regardless. Who you were is still a part of you, waiting on your own forgiveness to heal. There is no need for regret. When you come to love all of you, even the parts you once wished you could go back and change, you begin to smile gently and more tenderly at your humanness.

From this place, you can move forward with clearer certainty of who you are, drawing on courage to be more honest with yourself and others, drawing on faith and hope when challenged, and drawing on compassion and gratitude to create new directions.

Regret is a painful, self-condemning place. It does not need to be visited again if you are able to move forward now from a more gentle position of acceptance, kindness, and love. It is possible to live and to die without regrets. Your tender heart is waiting. Give it love, too.

ACKNOWLEDGMENTS

I feel gratitude for every step of my life that has led up to this point and will lead on beyond. I also feel gratitude for every person along the way who has influenced the journey, whether they are conscious of it or not. I especially feel gratitude to God, for giving me strength and teaching me the power of faith through consistent loving guidance.

Some people who have played a special role in my writing journey deserve a special mention: To my daughter and mother for bonding in such a wonderful way that I could sit quietly and write, leaving you both to mischief. To Leon Nacson, Managing Director of Hay House Australia, for the role of mentor in the book-publishing industry and for being so delightfully unique. To all of the Hay House team globally for the support of my author's journey. To friends and family for love and acceptance. And heartfelt thanks to all of the readers who connect positively with my work. Knowing that such like-minded souls are on the earth takes the feeling of "work" out of my actual work. Thank you all for the connection we share.

ABOUT
THE AUTHOR

Bronnie Ware is an author, songwriting teacher, and speaker from Australia. Her inspiring memoir, *The Top Five Regrets of the Dying,* has connected with hearts all over the world, with translations in 27 languages. Bronnie loves balance, simple living, health-loving food, and waking up to the songs of birds.

NOTES

NOTES

NOTES

NOTES

We hope you enjoyed this Hay House book. If you'd like to receive our online catalog featuring additional information on Hay House books and products, or if you'd like to find out more about the Hay Foundation, please contact:

Hay House, Inc., P.O. Box 5100, Carlsbad, CA 92018-5100
(760) 431-7695 or (800) 654-5126
(760) 431-6948 (fax) or (800) 650-5115 (fax)
www.hayhouse.com® • www.hayfoundation.org

Published and distributed in Australia by: Hay House Australia Pty. Ltd., 18/36 Ralph St., Alexandria NSW 2015 • *Phone:* 612-9669-4299 *Fax:* 612-9669-4144 • www.hayhouse.com.au

Published and distributed in the United Kingdom by: Hay House UK, Ltd., Astley House, 33 Notting Hill Gate, London W11 3JQ • *Phone:* 44-20-3675-2450 • *Fax:* 44-20-3675-2451 • www.hayhouse.co.uk

Published and distributed in the Republic of South Africa by: Hay House SA (Pty), Ltd., P.O. Box 990, Witkoppen 2068 *Phone/Fax:* 27-11-467-8904 • www.hayhouse.co.za

Published in India by: Hay House Publishers India, Muskaan Complex, Plot No. 3, B-2, Vasant Kunj, New Delhi 110 070 *Phone:* 91-11-4176-1620 • *Fax:* 91-11-4176-1630 • www.hayhouse.co.in

Distributed in Canada by: Raincoast Books, 2440 Viking Way, Richmond, B.C. V6V 1N2 • *Phone:* 1-800-663-5714 *Fax:* 1-800-565-3770 • www.raincoast.com

Take Your Soul on a Vacation

Visit www.HealYourLife.com® to regroup, recharge, and reconnect with your own magnificence. Featuring blogs, mind-body-spirit news, and life-changing wisdom from Louise Hay and friends.

Visit www.HealYourLife.com today